MEAT AROUND the BONE COMMUNICATION

MEAT AROUND

— THE —

BONE

COMMUNICATION

A NEW RELATIONSHIP PLAYBOOK

TO HELP YOU CLOSE MORE SALES, MAKE MORE FRIENDS

AND SPICE UP YOUR MARRIAGE

Jay R. Pocius

with Andy Earle

Copyright © 2020 by Jay R. Pocius

All rights reserved. No part of this book may be reproduced, distributed, or transmitted in any form or by any means, including photocopying, recording, or other electronic or mechanical methods, without the prior written permission of the author, except by a reviewer who may quote brief passages in promotion or in a review for this book and its contents.

Some names and identifying details have been changed to protect the privacy of individuals.

ISBN 979-8-218-50997-2

"To everyone who helped me see the need for a deeper level of communication in my life, I am forever grateful."

Contents

My Michael Jordan Moment

There is a specific type of communication that creates massive results when you apply it to your business and personal life. I first discovered the art of Meat Around the Bone Communication when I landed a cutthroat job selling life insurance door-to-door in college. Then, in my twenties, I perfected this communication in business while working at PNC Investments and I became one of their leading financial advisors. However, I didn't grasp the full importance of Meat Around the Bone Communication in my personal relationships until it was too late…

Early 2018 my engagement fell apart. I moved out of the condo I owned with my fiancé, Laurel, and into a dark, drafty, 300 square foot apartment on the north side of Chicago. That same year, I found out Samantha was pregnant with my son. And on top of that, I had to pay for the wedding that never happened.

The stress was so intense it felt like a physical weight was pressing in on me from all sides.

As I sat in my tiny kitchen, I got out a plate, bowl, cup, spatula, fork, and spoon. *I'm only going to be here for a couple months,* I told myself. *There's no need to unpack.*

It was the lowest I've ever felt.

Sitting there that first night in my shitty little apartment surrounded by boxes, I had a moment of self-realization. It drove me to change who I was. I vowed to communicate with Meat Around the Bone.

My discovery of Meat Around the Bone Communication didn't happen that night. It started seven years earlier when I was first hired as a financial advisor for PNC Investments. I was bouncing around jobs at the time. In less than two years I'd gone from Edward Jones to J.P.Morgan Chase to PNC Investments. I was hungry for work, but I was all over the place. I wasn't steady or reliable.

That's when a wholesaler pulled me aside and gave me the best advice I ever received: "You have to stay put," he said. "The top rule as an advisor is *stay put.* The longer you stay, the more business will come."

So when I came to PNC I knew I wanted to rebrand myself in a more steady, professional manner. That was the birth of Meat Around the Bone. I vowed to myself that I was going to be more organized, more efficient with my time, and a better communicator. To solidify that promise, I changed my name from Jayson to 'Jay.'

And I added my middle initial: *Jay R. Pocius.*

The new name was in my email signature. It was printed on my business cards. It was carved on the door of my office. It was a way of solidifying the change I wanted to make.

And it was working. As my success grew with PNC, others started wanting to learn what I was doing. Soon I was training every new financial advisor who joined our team. Then I was training most new advisors in the city of Chicago. All of a sudden, advisors from all over the Midwest Market were spending a full week with me learning how to better run their businesses. My Meat Around the Bone Communication was paying off and I was attracting attention.

Back in 1982, there was another kid who changed his name in order to make a promise to himself. An 18 year-old named Mike Jordan was playing basketball at the University of North Carolina. They made it to the national championship that year and Mike hit the game winning shot. In the aftermath of that moment he changed his name. He started referring to himself as 'Michael' Jordan instead of Mike. That shot gave him the confidence to become a legend over the next 16 years.

Changing the name on my business card was my way of saying, "Game on."

It was my Michael Jordan Moment.

Don't wait for your important relationships to fall apart like I did before you learn and apply Meat Around the Bone Communication.

Three years ago I would have told you there was nothing I needed to work on. I was killing it in my career, getting into real estate investing, and engaged to be married. I thought I had everything going on. In reality, it was the start of my downfall. Soon after that, my poor communication drove a wedge between my fiancé and I. We realized we weren't the same people who first fell in love. Our affection dwindled, life took its toll, and emotions between us grew cold and distant.

If you're completely satisfied with your communication right now, *fantastic.* I'm glad you're in a good place with all of your work and personal relationships. But stay alert. You never know what's coming around the corner.

Implementing Meat Around the Bone Communication is easy. Once you start, you will see improvements in your relationships across the board. Simply changing my business card was enough to start the process for me. It was a commitment to always leave some Meat Around the Bone, and a visual reminder of how I needed to change. As my business grew and I started receiving awards and promotions, it all felt like a confirmation of the new me. Meat Around the Bone Communication was working.

Today my new behavior is habitual. In all my professional interactions, Communicating with Meat Around the Bone is second nature. Now I'm making a new commitment to start systematically applying these same strategies in my personal relationships. This book is my way of putting that promise on paper. It's another Michael Jordan Moment.

I hope it will be helpful for you as well.

In these pages you'll learn the very best communication tools I've developed over the past ten years. You'll see how I use the power of Time Blocking to make sure everyone who contacts me hears back in less than 24 hours. I'll also show you my famous 1-2 punch to double your email response rate. And you'll see the ultimate strategy for responding to emotional voicemails and text messages (which has never failed me). Plus, I'll reveal how I ensure absolute success in my communication every day by what I do the *night before.*

But first, in Chapter 1, I'll explain the basics of Meat Around the Bone Communication and how it works…

Part 1

Chapter 1
Skin and Bones

Imagine you won the lottery this morning, received a check for $12 million, and drove straight to my office. I'm your financial advisor. You didn't call me before coming over. You were *so excited*, you weren't thinking straight. All you knew was you had to show me that check.

Tears well up in your eyes as you sprint through the lobby of my building and into the elevator.

On the ride up to my floor you realize your hands are shaking. This little piece of paper is the embodiment of all your hopes, dreams, and plans. As the door opens you race down the hallway to my office, remembering the countless hours we've spent together talking about your finances and your future. This check changes everything and there's nobody you are more excited to share the news with than me.

"Surprise!" you exclaim, slamming the check down on my desk with a triumphant grin. "How would you recommend we invest this check…for *twelve million dollars?*"

Think about how you would expect me to respond to this question.

I'd probably say something like:

"WHAT? I'm speechless. This is so exciting! How did this happen? Want to grab lunch and you can tell me all about it? *Hey, Mike, get in here! You have to see this right away, you're going to flip out!*"

Or maybe I would say:

"Words cannot begin to express how unbelievably happy I am for you right now. I am so touched, honored, and grateful that you came here first to share this with me."

Perhaps I would cry. Maybe I'd race around the desk and hug you. Or I might sit there for twenty seconds with my jaw hanging open, stammering nonsense as I try to wrap my head around what's going on.

The only thing I can guarantee I would not do is immediately answer your question about how to invest the check. You didn't come to my office to ask that question. You came to share your excitement. You knew I would understand exactly what you were feeling. Maybe you wanted to tell me immediately so you wouldn't be tempted to start spending the cash.

You wanted me to respond to your excitement, not to your actual question. Imagine how strange and cold it would feel if I said:

"Thirty-five percent private equity, thirty percent income-producing real estate, and a mix of public securities, high-yield corporate bonds, and emergency cash. You can leave the check with Mike on your way out. Bye."

If I responded like that, I wouldn't be your advisor for much longer. You'd find someone else to share your excitement (and money) with.

That's because there's no Meat Around the Bone in that type of answer. Yes, it's perfectly logical. But it's not very *human*. In fact, it misses the entire point of why you drove to my office in the first place. If all you cared about was depositing the money you could have simply mailed me the check with a note saying 'invest this.'

Meat Around the Bone Communication is about taking care of a person's *emotional* needs in addition to their *material* needs. It's about looking beyond what the person is saying and addressing why they're saying it.

If you're not addressing the other person's emotions first in every conversation, then your communication is all skin and bones.

I used this example to start the chapter because it makes the concept obvious, but many times the Meat Around the Bone response is challenging to figure out. In fact, it took me over a decade of constant practice to fully appreciate the intricacies of using Meat Around the Bone Communication to build stronger relationships with my clients. And I'm only beginning to unlock the power of this approach in my personal life.

Meat Around the Bone Communication is the art of getting your message across to the receiver while making them feel comfortable and at ease. It's about going the extra mile to make sure your message is delivered in the most appropriate way, instead of saying words haphazardly and hoping for the best. It's about being upfront with your expectations and explaining why you're asking certain questions. It's also about voicing appreciation when someone feels comfortable enough to divulge personal feelings and information.

My own education in Meat Around the Bone Communication started when I came to PNC Investments and met my mentor, Dmitry. He taught me how to have a full and meaningful conversation with a client. Every day we role played client interactions. We drilled scenarios repeatedly and no matter how many times we practiced Dmitry would always give me the same feedback:

I needed more meat around the bone. I needed to show more

concern for the human being I was talking to. I had to ask more personal questions rather than financial questions. Dmitry pushed me to communicate with my clients on a deeper level. I soon learned going deeper is the key to earning people's business.

Let's Get Emotional for a Minute

People throw the phrase 'meat on the bone' around in various contexts. In terms of a conversation it's about making people feel seen, heard, and special. When you take a genuine interest in someone's personal life they start to feel like you're their friend, like you see them as more than a business associate, that's Meat Around the Bone.

To this day, whenever I'm working on an important email I always send a draft to my partner, Mike, with the same question: "Do I have enough meat around the bone?"

You can incorporate more meat into nearly every conversation you have. Showing appreciation when people share their feelings goes a long way. This practice takes time to internalize.

I talk to people *all day long.* Whether I'm on the phone or in meetings, I am always talking to someone. So when I finally shut down for the day and start to decompress I really don't want to talk to anyone anymore. With my ex fiancé, Laurel, that was exactly when she wanted to connect with me. When I came home after a day at the office, my Meat Around the Bone mindset went completely out the window. I became direct and easily irritated. That spelled the beginning of the end.

Think about it this way: You might be exhausted at the end of the day and not have energy left to take a call from a friend. But maybe that person waited all day to call you because they knew you were busy at work. And now you're going to be an ass and shut them down? They might start to wonder why they even bother checking in with you at all.

Long term relationships of any kind are important. It shocks me when I hold joint appointments with other advisors and potential clients. Often, as soon as we sit down and introduce ourselves the other advisor will dive straight into financial questions. And these are *seasoned* advisors.

I usually have to say, "Hold on, let's pause here. Back it up a second. The whole point of this meeting is to learn about the client."

When you sit down in front of me or another financial advisor, you're not there to order a new debit card or ask if I can waive an overdraft fee. If you were, a surface-level interaction could be acceptable. But investing, financial planning, and your retirement are not small conversations. That's important stuff! So I want my conversations to be as full and complete as possible.

Even if the client doesn't know the answers to all of my questions, I want to make them think about their life in ways they have never thought about it before. *Wow, he's really asking deep questions.* In my mind, if I'm not having a deep conversation, I'm doing the client a disservice.

Plus, going deep can make you more money.

Today at my firm, J.M.Equity Advisors, Mike and I always look for ways to add more meat to the bone. Every conversation we have comes from a financial planning standpoint and we are committed to making sure we ask about every detail, no matter how small. Our clients all know and trust us personally.

There are many clients I inherited from other advisors at PNC, and when I started having deep conversations with them I often uncovered assets the previous advisor never found. I have grown $50,000 relationships to $500,000, and then to $1 million and more using this kind of conversation. Many people have never had a financial conversation like this. A full financial planning conversation is deep. It entails asking a lot of questions and learning every possible financial detail about the client, regardless of how big or small the opportunity is.

I want to unearth every opportunity for business. I will often turn my computer screens around and show people everything that goes into a financial plan, walking them through my software, and showing them exactly the kind of information I'm putting in. The idea is that my client and I are doing this together, and they love it. They can see projections for how long their money will last, as well as what happens when we make their strategy more conservative or aggressive.

Once people see what I'm seeing, they are more inclined to answer all my questions because they want accurate information. By explaining why I'm asking certain questions, instead of just jumping in and asking them, I'm communicating with Meat Around the Bone.

As my firm hires more people, the Meat Around the Bone concept is becoming our signature. I intend to make it central to our corporate culture. It will be my biggest teaching point to help my employees expand their client relationships.

The way you sell is the way you communicate, and you're always selling something. Therefore, sales is all about Meat Around the Bone Communication. To be successful, you want to make people comfortable by connecting emotionally and addressing the emotions behind their responses.

Every successful salesperson knows you're supposed to sell based on emotion. They say buying is 90% emotional and 10% logical. Facts are certainly important, but feelings trump facts any day.

Your communication should be no different when you're trying to make sales at home. You need to focus on why the other person is saying what they're saying. The words alone won't tell you enough.

For example, if a conversation evolves into an argument, step back and take a deep breath. Slow things down. In the heat of the moment, no one's ever logical. It's all emotion. We sell based on emotion and resolve based on logic. So when a significant other disagrees with you, don't immediately fire back your response. Look for the emotion behind their statements.

Dive into why they are acting this way, and address their feelings.

There are times when a client will email me and get straight to the point. Maybe they're concerned about something. *We need to talk about this right away.* When I get those kinds of emails I don't answer immediately, because my first instinct is usually to get snappy. I've learned firing back an emotional response escalates the issue without solving it.

When I got my first sales job in college, I was very direct with customers. If someone hung up on me I would call them right back. Oddly enough they would answer. I would say, "I know you didn't just hang up on me, because that would be rude. I'm hoping the call just dropped. OK, as I was saying…"

That directness doesn't fly as a financial advisor. I've learned to be more tactful. When a client emails me something infuriating today, I will purposely delay my response. I'll wait until I've calmed down, and when I do respond I'll start off with some meat:

"Hey, hope you're enjoying the day. Thank you for following up with me. I appreciate the fact that you feel comfortable enough to reach out and voice your concerns. I've done my best to address your comments below. At the end of the day if you don't feel 100% comfortable, I'm not doing my job as a financial advisor. So I hope this makes sense. How about I give you a call? Is tomorrow at 8am alright?"

Note that I haven't rushed to answer their pressing concern. I am responding to the subtext behind what they asked me. No matter what the issue is, I say I'm glad they feel comfortable reaching out to me because, really I am glad. I would much rather have them tell me about their concerns so I can address them rather than keep quiet and start seeking a new advisor. My priority is to make the client feel cared for.

Honestly, the investment part of my job is easy. The relationships are the challenge. There's a reason Mike and I call ourselves 'relationship managers.' The way we see it, we're not money managers or stock pickers. Relationships are the foundation of everything we do. No matter what investing I do for a client, at the end of the day it all comes down to communicating with Meat Around the Bone.

When an angry client calls, 99% of the time you don't have to make any changes to their accounts. But you can't say, "Everything is fine, stop freaking out." That's not very tactful. You need Meat Around the Bone. You need to make them *feel* good. You might have already thought about all the pros and cons of a particular choice, but the client hasn't and immediate results can put them in an emotionally-charged state. It's your responsibility to calm them down. Then you can walk them through your thought process.

Emotion first, logic later.

If you've gone to therapy, you know therapists don't come right out with answers. Instead, during a session, they might pause here and there to explain why they're asking certain questions. Ultimately, the goal is for you to come to your own realization of what's wrong. The therapist's job is to guide you there. The answers all come from you.

I always ask people *why* they invested in specific funds. "Who recommended this? What fees are you paying to be in these funds?" I make people think.

The angry client isn't emailing because you need to make

changes to their accounts. They're emailing for confirmation that previous changes were the right ones. *Why did we do that again?*

You don't need to immediately come back and say, "Sorry, let's change it back." Instead, give them a call and talk through their concerns to find out what's really going on.

If you don't, then two months later during the next market swing they'll want to make another change. But the reason behind the change is something that's making them uncomfortable. Your email should be constructed to make them comfortable. Don't immediately agree to the change. Focus on making them feel comfortable reaching out to you, comfortable with their portfolio, and comfortable trusting you to make the best decision and provide the best advice moving forward.

Make People Feel Comfortable, Not Stupid

One thing I got wrong in my relationship with Laurel, was I often focused on the words she was saying instead of looking beneath the words to her feelings. When she came to me with an issue, maybe something that happened at work or with a friend, my first response was often to tell her how to solve the problem.

"Why don't you just...?"

I now realize I was making her feel stupid. The subtext of my remark was, *Why did you ask me this dumb question? I solved it in merely four seconds. You must be really dense.*

That's not Meat Around the Bone. That's not emotional care. What Laurel needed was an empathetic conversation, but I cut her off at the knees and didn't engage with her feelings. I responded to the pure facts. It made her feel stupid for even mentioning it. Pretty soon she didn't want to tell me about her day or her problems anymore.

What I failed to say was…

- "I'm glad you feel comfortable talking through this with me."
- "That sounds really frustrating."
- "I see your point of view."
- "I see why you responded this way."
- "How did that make you feel?"
- "Let's think about this."
- "Something similar happened to me and it made me feel terrible."
- "Let's figure out the best way to address this together."

That's a different kind of conversation than telling her what to do. These Meat Around the Bone phrases have nothing to do with the actual content of what she said. They are about emotional care.

The same has been true with my son's mother, Samantha. When I ask about her new job, or about her friends, she gives me very short answers because she's afraid to open up to me. I don't blame her. She's been burned too many times by my poor communication.

For some reason I'm much better about this with my clients. I am patient and I consistently put Meat Around the Bone. I ask questions, I explain why I ask them, and I lead people to discover the answers to their financial questions for themselves.

I now need to do the same for Samantha and everyone else in my personal life. I need to expand this beyond work. I don't want conversations to feel confrontational. People should feel like I'm on their team and I care about their problems, not just solutions.

Approach every interaction with the attitude that the two of you are on the same team. This really helps. When someone comes to you and they are upset, look past the words and try to read the subtext. Go deeper and collaborate.

You can often tell when your significant other has had a shitty day at work. When their aggravation boils over and they start complaining, take a step back. If you retaliate with your emotions, an argument is bound to escalate. Avoid pouring gasoline on the fire. Try following these three simple steps:

1. Slow down and take a deep breath.
2. Ask questions to get to the root of what the person is feeling.
3. Now solve the problem together.

It's the artful way of responding. Ask questions and get a full understanding of their concerns.

Communication is the glue that holds every relationship together. Happiness in life boils down to good communication. And good communication comes down to how much meat you put on the bone.

The right level of meat will depend on the person. I have some clients who like a lot of meat on the bone. For these types of people, I might spend as much as 90% of a meeting chatting about personal stuff and slip the business items in where I can. On the other hand, I have clients who prefer straightforwardness and want me to get to the point after a few minutes of chitchat. Nailing this balance is the art.

Regardless, every conversation should start with Meat Around the Bone. For the more direct individuals, the 'meat' might be a chat about the reason for meeting, almost like the intro to a book.

No book is going to start right off with Chapter 1 out of nowhere. You have to ease the reader in with an intro. "Hey, thanks for coming. Now here's what we're gonna be talking about…"

If the other person isn't prone to opening up, you can take the initiative.

With Laurel, I stopped communicating deeply with her and sharing my feelings. I resisted voicing how much I appreciated when she shared her thoughts. I stopped voicing my love for her, except for a simple, "I love you." And it took its toll on our relationship. We drifted apart. We became aggravated with each other. We stopped communicating in a positive way.

Instead of pressing in and strengthening our relationship, we slowly turned our attention elsewhere. This problem perpetuated into my next relationship.

I can be very short with Samantha. I often don't take an interest in her and I don't share much of my professional or personal life with her. It leaves our relationship cold, even when we're together. We're both loving to our son, Jayden, but over the last few years I've learned that my communication towards her was wrong in every way, and it's something I vow to fix moving forward.

Failing to incorporate Meat Around the Bone Communication in conversations diminishes your relationships. Conversely, by practicing Meat Around the Bone in every conversation, you'll be strengthening your connections with others.

Dmitry, my mentor back at PNC, told me home is the best place for him to practice having conversations the right way. He liked to practice conversation skills with his niece, who was five or six years old. He practiced conversing with her every day, and it showed up in his work and in his adult relationships.

I have failed at this in my personal life.

I want to be like Dmitry and have Meat Around the Bone conversations in my personal life. I've started implementing some tactics into personal conversations, especially uncomfortable ones. One tactic, for example, is purposely asking lots of questions to get to the root of the initial statement.

With Samantha, I now try to focus on uncovering what she's really telling me. When I adopt this mindset I find conversations are easier and less likely to turn confrontational.

I also purposely pause before I reply. This allows me to calm down in those initial seconds. This dramatically helps me in my responses to pointed statements. The pause doesn't have to be long. Mine are typically 3 to 5 seconds. Those few seconds remind me to respond with calm, Meat Around the Bone statements. I also find pauses help defuse situations. Samantha can see I'm taking the time to think about my responses, and she knows I'm doing my part to keep the conversations constructive.

Additionally, I now make it a point to tell Samantha right off the bat that although this is an uncomfortable topic and I am feeling anxiety on the inside, I am making the effort to have the conversation and to fully participate in this relationship so we can resolve the issue at hand. This type of statement not only acknowledges my effort and transparency, it helps me navigate the conversation in a constructive way that ultimately strengthens the relationship.

I now spend the weekends with Samantha and my son, and I've been making a habit of leaving my laptop at home when I go over to her place. I used to bring my laptop, but work has a way of popping up if I have a computer handy, so now I leave it at home. This forces me to be fully present. I also turn notifications off on my phone, and I keep it off my body. I might check it a couple of times if I have some space to myself, but my main focus is to spend time with Jayden and Samantha.

In this chapter we've looked at the basics of Meat Around the Bone Communication and how it shows up in your personal and professional relationships. But what about brand new acquaintances who you don't have a strong relationship with yet? In Chapter 2 I'll show you how I use Meat Around the Bone to grow new relationships and move them to the next level…

Chapter 2

Fattening Up

In business and in life there will always be people who you are working on moving up to the next level. Maybe you've got a prospect who you'd like to turn into a client, a boyfriend or girlfriend you'd like to make into your fiancé, or an acquaintance who you're interested in escalating to the status of a close friend. But the relationship doesn't seem to be moving forward as fast as you'd like.

There will often be a string of obstacles when you're trying to escalate a relationship. In fact, other people may subconsciously throw obstacles in your way because they want to test you and make sure you're going to stick around. They're trying to determine whether you're worthy of their business, friendship, or love before they give it to you.

This chapter is about the art of relationship escalation. We're going to talk about how to Fatten Up your communication and create a feeling of forward momentum and progress. I'll show you how to put some juicy, marbled, tender meat around the bone to get people leaning in and asking for more. Fattening Up your communication is the key to escalating any kind of relationship to the next level.

This chapter is about building trust. Trust is the foundation of strong relationships. In business, when others deeply trust you, deals seem to close themselves. In personal life, trust encourages friends and lovers to escalate relationships with you.

My general philosophy is that anybody who agrees to let me follow up with them will eventually do business with me someday. I strive to have better follow up than any other financial advisor out there. Following up properly is the secret to Fattening Up your communication and building trust quickly.

The first annuity I ever sold required a *lot* of follow-up. I wasn't familiar with annuities at the time, so I didn't know what I was talking about when one potential client asked me to explain the benefits of a certain equity-indexed annuity. As I was walking Charley through the annuity and explaining the benefits, he asked a question I didn't know the answer to. Instead of making something up I told him I wasn't sure, but that I would find out the answer and report back within a couple of days.

Next, I got in touch with the carrier who held the annuity and I gathered the information he wanted to know. Then I called Charley up again and told him what I'd learned. But as we were talking, he had another question I didn't know the answer to. So, again, I promised to do research and get in touch with him as soon as I found out. I then went and made another call to the carrier.

This cycle repeated itself *thirteen times.* Each time I found an answer to Charley's question he stumped me with a new one on the next call. Finally, after six weeks of these back and fourths, he ran out of questions, and I knew everything there was to know about equity-indexed annuities.

Charley told me he was ready to move forward. He bought the annuity and to this day he's still a client of mine. Because of that experience, I now know I can always find the information I need if I look hard enough. More importantly, I saw the Meat Around the Bone power of following up to build trust and escalate a relationship.

There is nothing more important in business than good follow-up. It's the key to success because it strengthens trust, and trust moves relationships forward. As a financial advisor, I have plenty of competition. There's a financial advisor on every block in America. Other firms are offering the same investments at the same price. We might have slightly different strategies, but the service we provide is the same.

So how do you decide which advisor you want to trust your life savings to?

It's all about personal connection. As an advisor, people invest in *you*. My clients like knowing I'm always going to act in a fiduciary capacity and that they can trust me to follow up and make the changes that need to be made based on whatever is happening in the market. They're investing in me.

Having solid follow-up is the best way to prove yourself to people and win their business. When they see how well you follow up with them, prospects will learn they can trust you to do what you say you will in a professional, assertive manner. As a result, they will turn into clients.

When you try to schedule a meeting with someone and they tell you it's not a very good time, don't give up on that person entirely. Simply move them forward another week or two on your calendar and follow up with them to see if it's a better time.

Fattening Up your communication is about looking for every possible excuse to remember something important about someone. Remembering little details builds trust. There's no shortage of things to remember about someone. Birthdays are great. You can remember their birthday, kids' birthdays, spouse's birthday, and major events, like purchasing or selling a home, or retiring.

Work hard to remember those things and follow back with people about them. Don't neglect people because they don't give you a 'yes' right off the bat.

Trust means the world to clients and prospects, and it also means the world to your family. Nobody likes to feel unimportant.

Remember to Escalate

Allison was a client of mine at PNC and I'm still trying to get her to move her accounts over to my new firm. She is a busy attorney and I've been trying to schedule a conversation with her, but every time I reach out she tells me it's not a good time. Then she said her brother contracted COVID and he was in the hospital. She told me she's not making financial decisions and her mind is focused on her family and her work.

I waited a few weeks and reached again and she told me she was still in the same position. So I added her to my calendar to follow up with again in a few weeks. And when I do I will be sure to ask about her brother and how her family is doing before I even mention the possibility of having a financial conversation.

She has been in my pipeline for quite some time and I've been gradually Fattening Up my communication with her to move her toward escalating our relationship. Depending on the nature of the sales cycle in your industry you might have prospects in your pipeline for many months. Following back with these people regularly is key to moving them toward an eventual sale.

Another potential client, a married couple, is currently in my pipeline getting Fattened Up as well. When I met with them a couple months ago they were ready to move forward and start setting up accounts. They mentioned their big goal is to move out of their apartment in the city and get a house in the suburbs. I asked when they thought that might happen and they said they were already looking for houses every weekend, all day Saturday and Sunday. This search was serious.

"Realistically speaking," I said, "what if you found a house this weekend? You'd go under contract and start speaking to a mortgage person and giving them documents. And the last thing they want is to see money movement. They hate that. They need to see statements showing the titling was the same. It can be a pain in the ass. If we move your accounts over this week it's going to take a full month before your first statement is generated. So if you guys are this serious about finding a house, I would say we hold off and do it once you close the deal. The last thing I want to do is complicate the situation for you."

This couple was grateful that I put their long term interests first and helped them see the big picture, and as a financial advisor I believe that's my job.

Since then I've reached out and continued to follow up. And for a while they said they were still looking. But eventually they found a house. Recently I followed back with them again asking if they ever closed on the house. They said, "Yes! So let's get together at the end of June to revisit our conversation."

That's a great example of following back. I purposely didn't try to push for the business because I knew it wouldn't benefit them. But the fact that I eased off and told them it was in their best interest to wait demonstrated a lot of value. I look forward to meeting and having a conversation with them about becoming clients.

Until then, I will continue to follow up with them at every opportunity until they decide to move over the accounts.

Short On Fat

Failing to follow up can cause your relationships to wither and die. That's what happened to a contractor I was planning to hire a few months ago.

My loft here in Chicago has really high ceilings (23 feet to be exact). My initial plan was to build a second story before I moved in. I met with a couple contractors while I was looking at buying the place and got bids for what I wanted to do. They came and looked at the unit and said they would follow up with a rough ballpark of what it might possibly cost. The contractor I really liked came in a few different times and brought plumbers and electricians to make sure we could do a bathroom upstairs.

The next step was to have his architect come in and draw up some plans.

I really liked this contractor because he was a great sales guy. He communicated with Meat Around the Bone. If he would have been a financial advisor I would have tried to hire him! But for some reason he stopped following up with me. He never Fattened me Up! Every time I got a hold of him he told me how busy he was. Eventually, our communication fell apart.

A couple months later, after the COVID pandemic set in, he called me saying he was starved for business and asking when we could get started. He said he was ready to send the architect over that same week. But with coronavirus in full swing and me stuck at home all day, it wasn't a good time for a remodel. I told him I was going to have to wait.

He missed out on a sizable project because he didn't follow up and close the deal. And when the virus dies down and I do start the second floor addition, I'll probably hire a different contractor.

The outcome may have been different if this contractor kept his promises and routinely followed up with me as intended. Instead of Fattening me Up he allowed our relationship to starve and die. The trust I had for him evaporated. Due to his lack of follow-up, I honestly don't trust him to complete all the work on time as promised. No one likes collaborating with someone who can't follow through on their commitments. And as expected, this expands beyond the work setting.

While my follow-up skills are immaculate when it comes to my business, I often catch myself neglecting to Fatten Up my relationships with friends and family members. Those relationships are prone to starve, especially when work gets busy. I recently noticed I was following up better with other advisors I'm considering hiring than with my own family.

In my line of work, the quickest way to exponentially grow your firm is to hire advisors who already have a steady book of business. Growing the firm is my number one priority right now. It's much easier to hire someone who can bring a hundred million dollars worth of assets to your firm than it is to find a hundred million dollars in assets yourself.

I realized during the coronavirus pandemic, while the entire world was on lockdown, I was still finding time to text and email advisors I'm trying to recruit: "Hey, hope you're safe. Hope your family's doing well. I look forward to speaking with you once this is all done."

But I wasn't following up with people in my personal life in the same way. That's a big problem because after several attempts to connect with you, if people feel they are being ignored and pushed off they will stop trying.

Of course, many of my friends and family members did come to me and ask how everything was going with the pandemic. "How are you and Mike doing with everything going on in the market? Are you guys surviving? How's Jayden?"

I never reciprocated that. I answered when others reached out to me, but I never asked of others myself. I failed to Fatten Up those relationships. Now, I need to find a way to put some more Meat Around the Bone.

My lack of personal follow-up is baffling because I've seen its benefits first hand in my professional life. It's been eight months now since Mike and I went out on our own to start J.M.Equity Advisors. We knew going into this that follow-up was going to be critical. We had a deliver-or-die mentality because we weren't get-ting a steady income anymore. The only way we would make any money during those first few months was by moving our clients over. And many of the clients that I anticipated moving over quick-ly ended up taking a few months to make a decision. Those clients tested my level of follow-up and attentiveness, even though I'd proven it before. After years of constant communication, the relationships still needed more Fattening Up before the clients could make such a big leap.

Eight months later Mike and I have moved over more clients than we ever hoped. And when a client makes the decision to bring their relationship to our firm, the feeling of success and accomplishment is so great because it's *our* firm. These people transferred their accounts to work with *us* and not a bank. Follow-up is the reason they trust us.

Put a lot of Meat Around the Bone. Fatten Up. It will pay off.

That being said, you can't get lazy once someone becomes a client, friend, lover, or spouse. You can't start slacking on your follow-up because as soon as you do, the relationship will starve. As a fiduciary, my clients pay me an annual fee to manage their accounts. By law I have to meet with them at least once per year to review their accounts and positions. If I don't do that, I'm not doing my job as a financial advisor. I often see advisors get complacent and stop doing these pesky financial plans. That might work for a few years, but eventually their clients start looking elsewhere for an advisor who makes them feel listened to and cared for.

If you don't put the Meat Around the Bone, people will find someone else who does. Nobody likes skin-and-bones relationships.

When someone becomes my client, I continue to pepper them with constant touches. One thing I make sure to do is send people personalized mail. Yes, snail mail. I hand write cards for all of my clients on their birthdays, holidays, and special occasions. I also reach out to them with helpful information, to make small changes to their accounts, and to ask if they need anything from me. I work to keep all of my client relationships Fattened Up and marbled so that everyone feels financially, and emotionally, cared for. We'll get into the logistics of this in the next chapter…

Chapter 3

Maintaining Muscle Mass

For the relationships in your life that you're not currently attempting to escalate, you'll want to shift them into Maintenance Mode. It's similar to the world of weight lifting. For instance, I've currently reached this point in my relationship with my thighs where I'd like to maintain them at the current size. My biceps could probably never get too big, but my thighs have plenty of Meat Around the Bone right now and if they get any bigger I'd have to go up a pants size—not optimal.

That's why weightlifters talk about switching your workouts from a *hypertrophy* focus (gaining size and strength) to a *muscle maintenance* focus. Relationships are exactly the same way. Once you've escalated your connection with someone to the point where you're happy with the relationship, it's time to switch from Fattening Up to Muscle Maintenance.

The majority of your relationships are going to be in Maintenance Mode at any given time. Fattening someone Up takes a lot of energy and it's not practical to work on escalating too many people to a higher-level relationship simultaneously. While you're focusing on leveling up a few critical communication channels, it's important to make sure the other ones aren't starting to atrophy.

One illustrative example is my relationship with Francini, who was my assistant when I worked at PNC. Through years of daily collaboration she became integral to my business at PNC. Eventually, when my clients would call in, they enjoyed talking to her just as much as me. Now that I'm out on my own my clients are always asking me, "What's going on with Francini? Is she still at PNC? When are you going to hire her?"

Since I left PNC, our relationship has stayed strong. There is never more than a three-day span where one of us doesn't check in with the other. How is her house shopping going? How's her son, Lucas? How is Jayden, doing?

We follow up with each other constantly. This isn't motivated by self-interest. Neither of us is trying to get something from the other in return. We have that type of relationship that almost seems to maintain itself automatically.

(I wish the same could be said for my quads.)

Think of someone in your life who you follow up with automatically. They follow up with you out of habit and you get back to them because it feels effortless. For me, these people include Mike, Brennan, Elyse, and Francini. These people care about me and I care about them. We communicate naturally.

The goal with this chapter is to take the same types of strategies you're using naturally with your core friends and start applying them to everybody else. Stop allowing people to slip through the cracks. Prevent relationships from losing ground when they're not your central focus.

If one of your old high school friends texted you while you were in the middle of something important you probably wouldn't respond immediately. But that's OK, because they don't expect you to. The key is you need to get back to them in the next 24 hours. You can't ignore them.

There are some things you can do that don't require any extra time at all. For instance, any time I meet with a client, no matter what we talk about, I always wrap up the conversation by reviewing what we covered. Then I end with, "Is there anything more I can be doing as your financial advisor? Anything that's important to you or any concerns I'm not addressing?"

Even after our client appreciation event last year, I reached out to people and asked what they thought of the event, what their favorite part was, what they didn't like, and whether they made any interesting connections. Most said the event was fantastic, but I got a few clients who gave me good feedback, such as the quantity of standing tables versus sitting and the selection of drinks besides alcohol. This follow-up revealed an opportunity to improve future events, and was also a chance to maintain connection with everyone to keep the relationships strong.

In my business life, I am constantly reviewing my clients' accounts and ensuring I understand their goals. I'm on the phone with people every day checking in, and I always ask what I can do better. In my personal relationships, I don't do that. I figure, *everything's great.* But, of course, people are always going through change and having new experiences. They get new jobs, go back to school, have kids, get divorced, and start new relationships. There's always something new going on.

Mike is excellent at doing this kind of Meat Around the Bone Muscle Maintenance in the personal realm. He'll often end a conversation with me by saying, "Hey, let me know if you need anything." *Well yeah, duh. We've been friends forever and run a business together.* But he doesn't let me take that fact for granted. He's constantly putting in relational reassurances.

- "Let me know if you need anything."
- "Hey, if you need to talk I'm always here."
- "Can I do anything else for you at all?"

Hitting A Whole Flock of Birds at Once

Group events, like my client appreciation event, are a great way to touch a large number of people at once. You could host a regular party once a month and invite everybody you know. People don't have to come if they don't want to, but inviting them every month gives you a reason to connect with them and say, "Hey, how is everything going? I miss you! Having a little cocktail night on Saturday if you're in the area. Would be great to catch up :)"

You might consider starting a monthly wine or poker night. Some people use book clubs as an excuse to get together regularly with friends. It doesn't have to be extravagant, but find a way to bring everyone together and enjoy an evening once a month. It is a key strategy used by the top connectors.

If you don't want to host an event, there are other activities that can be fun. Ghost tours, a day at the beach, group cooking classes, party bus rentals, sports games, and annual vacations all come to mind. There are countless group activities you could initiate.

In the summer I play beach volleyball at North Avenue Beach here in Chicago. Each year the same group of friends comes together to play volleyball every Monday night after work. The funny thing is, I only see this specific group of friends when it's volleyball season. Outside of summer volleyball, we have never hung out. Although this may be viewed as a negative and a terrible lack of follow-up on my part, I refer to it here simply as a way to demonstrate the power of a group activity to bring people together regularly.

A Failure to Communicate

While my Muscle Maintenance is stellar in the business sphere, I often fail to adequately maintain my personal relationships. I tell myself I'm too busy. *I'm building a business.*

To be honest, this isn't a new development—I have a track record of brushing off friends or family if it means growing professionally. You might say I'm selfish and self-centered, and I'd agree with you. This way of conducting myself has developed me into the efficient sales person and business owner I am today.

But now I want more. I want to experience complete success in all aspects of my life. I'm not ashamed to say I've neglected and sacrificed personal relationships to ultimately get where I am today, and I'll admit that it has come at a cost. I have felt pain along the way, and I now understand that professional and personal growth go hand-in-hand. One cannot exist without the other.

When I go home my computer is still logged in. I'm still working. Maybe I'm spending time on LinkedIn looking for advisors to hire. I forget how important constantly touching people is on the personal side. If I continue putting that off, people are going to go away and not reach out to me anymore.

My personal relationships will lose muscle mass.

So I've started to closely examine the behaviors I exhibit in my professional life to maintain my relationships at a high level, and apply those same techniques to the personal side. For example, I have one client, a couple named John and Heather Camp that I've never met in person because they live in Michigan. I inherited them at PNC from another advisor less than six months before I left.

When I first inherited the Camps we had a call on which I introduced myself and asked a series of deep questions to learn about their accounts and their goals. We ended up making quite a few changes. I got the sense these accounts were moved to me because their previous advisor at PNC wasn't doing a very good job.

It seemed like I was on a positive path with this couple when, six months later, Mike and I started calling all of our clients to announce we'd left PNC and started our own practice.

When I got John and Heather on the phone they told me flat out they had no real allegiance to PNC. But still, they didn't immediately move their accounts over. It took about 2-3 months before they fully completed the transfer. Once we finally did move their accounts over they told me I followed up with them more in the two months it took for them to move their accounts over than anybody at PNC had ever touched them in the seven years they banked there. Because of all those touches and follow-ups they decided to move everything over!

We won that relationship in a little over two months, and I've never met them in person.

That blew me away.

Checking in with people regularly makes them feel special. It's my goal that no client ever feels forgotten about, or less important, than other clients. I often hear clients with smaller financial portfolios say, "I know I'm not as important as other clients, but thank you for doing what you do." I always assure them they are just as important as everyone else because it's a relationship business.

Even though smaller relationships bring in less immediate revenue than larger relationships, I've found smaller clients are significantly more likely to give you referrals. It's almost like they are subconsciously trying to make up for the fact that you treat them exactly the same as your biggest clients by sending you additional work.

So touching everybody is important. No client relationship is more important than the next.

When I first met Vivian we started with only $40,000 and I helped her to invest it. True to my Meat Around the Bone Communication style, I treated her with as much care and attention as my very biggest clients. And she noticed.

Turns out the $40k she'd given me wasn't her entire portfolio. It was a bit of extra cash she had lying around. When she saw the level of attentiveness I committed to maintain our relationship, $40k quickly became $150k. And then, pretty soon, $150k became $500k. From there Vivian gave me all her Morgan Stanley statements to review. I asked questions she didn't know the answers to. Then we went into a full financial plan, eventually moving over the entire relationship.

As we were moving the accounts over, her advisor at Morgan Stanley called and pleaded with Vivian not to move the money. He said his son was going to take over his business and she could work with him. Funny, she hadn't received a single call from him in over three years prior to that. His lack of attention had led to a major loss of muscle mass in their relationship. It didn't take much for me to swoop in with some Meat Around the Bone and win her business.

She ended up moving everything over. More than $2 million. Today, she's one of my largest clients. Her daughter, Natalie, is now a client of mine too.

That's what can happen when you treat every relationship as important.

By making constant touches and artfully addressing what's important to clients, you *win* their business. But in order to *keep* their business, you have to make them feel special.

If you get in touch with your client and they are appreciative and grateful, that's a great response. If they have questions and concerns, that might mean you need to increase your level of touches with that client. If they are annoyed, tone it down or adjust your strategy.

Every relationship will be different, but maintain constant touches with everybody.

One way I do this is with random check-in calls. I might know a certain client only wants to review their accounts every six months or once a year. And maybe the market is perfectly fine so there's not much to talk about—no real reason to call. But I'll still give them a call or shoot them an email to check in, see how everything is going, and answer any questions.

I also might randomly call or text clients and invite them to lunch or dinner. Most people say something along the lines of, "That sounds good! Let me get back to you when I'm not so busy." And then it never happens. But there are certain clients who *love* going to lunch. So I'll make sure to invite these people out because I know it makes them feel special.

The reality is they always want to pay for lunch too. So we end up switching off who takes the bill. It's become a way for them to show their appreciation for us.

It means a lot that my clients want to pay for lunch when I'm the one who invited them in the first place. It underscores the fact that they appreciate my constant touches and the mother-hen level of attention I give them. Relationships are two-way streets. My hope is always that my clients are as appreciative to have me as their advisor as I am to have them as a client.

Relationships are partnerships, and when you make someone feel special they will look for ways to reciprocate and show their appreciation in response. People love that I constantly reach out to them, invite them to lunch, and send them birthday cards in addition to managing their portfolios. They feel as appreciative of me and Mike as we do of them. We're both in this together.

Just because you already won business does not mean you

can stop following up with clients and reviewing their relationships and accounts. Do standard review calls every six months, or on an annual basis, whatever the client would prefer. But orchestrate in additional touches throughout the year. Take advantage of birthdays, holidays, and monthly emails.

You're always going to have family and friends with different life events happening. Follow back on these things and ask how they're going. Maintain the Muscle. How's the new job? How was the interview? How did the speech go? Follow back relentlessly.

Follow Back Relentlessly

Whereas following *up* is about keeping your word and getting back to people as promised, following *back* is about finding excuses to check back in with people even when there's no direct need to do so. It's the biggest secret to maintaining muscle mass in all of your relationships and making sure everyone stays excited about you.

There are so many times I've had prospects tell me they haven't talked to their advisor in years. That's ridiculous. Why would someone ever go out of their way to recommend you to others if you barely give them any attention? I don't want that to happen. I want my clients to feel compelled to talk about their experience with me because I've made them feel special. You'll never get re-ferrals if you don't constantly follow back with people.

You can never have too much follow back. Obviously you don't want to be annoying. But professionally, I don't think you can ever have too much. My clients get touched every single month. I have everybody set up on an automatic email newsletter that covers different topics. It's actually market updates put together by Wells Fargo and stapled with our firm name and logo, but it gives us a way to reach out to everyone.

Remembering big events carries weight, and it's easy. Birth-days happen once per year. The fact that I remember my clients', spouses', and kids' birthdays is above and beyond.

Following back can become too much if you're constantly do-ing the same thing on a regular basis. For example, don't ask how someone is doing every single day. Checking in on something specific is much better than saying, "Hey, how are you doing?" all the time. However, if you know someone is looking for a house, it's ok to check in consistently and see how their search is going, because that's specific. That's following back.

When there's an occasion, you can follow back about it of-ten. When there isn't, you can follow back by using phrases that don't require a response and, thus, don't indicate neediness. For instance:

- "I saw this meme and it made me think of you, for obvious reasons haha…Hope all is well."
- "Just a heads up I'm out of the office this week but I'll still be answering emails."
- "Ok, you were right, I did have to upgrade to the larger size…should have listened to you!"
- "Aloha, I'm back in the office and wanted to share a quick photo from our trip. Mahalo :)"

One of my best friends, Brennan, got laid off from his job a few weeks ago and when I found out I reached out to say, "Hey man, I'm so sorry. How are you doing with everything?" And he was actually very happy about it. He's getting unemployment and the time off allows him to browse new web development programs to hopefully make a career change in the near future. So that's great. But it gave me a reason to follow back.

A couple years ago, when Laurel and I lived together, we went to a big holiday party at our neighbor's house. And I met one of their close friends who's a financial advisor. She told me she only has 60 clients, but they're all big. And she doesn't accept any new clients. All she does is smother her current clients in service. She services them so well that if they ever had a conversation with another advisor, they would never even think about switching over.

But you don't necessarily want to 'smother' your friends and family members. One good way to Maintain Muscle without overwhelming people is simply to get better at remembering what you talked about the last time you saw someone.

There's a big difference between asking, "How's life?" and asking, "How's your final semester of school, is that capstone course as tough as you thought it would be?" This demonstrates that you paid close attention during your previous conversation. That means something because most of the time we are barely listening to the other person while we wait for our turn to speak.

Lead into conversations with something specific about the person you're talking to. In the business world, I am deliberate about remembering specifics because it makes a huge difference in client relationships. For instance, when I followed up with Allison, the high-powered attorney who I'm hoping to sign up soon as a client, I didn't talk business. Instead, I asked how her brother was doing since she'd told me previously he was in the hospital with COVID.

Something similar happened recently with one of my biggest clients, Vivian, because it's tax season. She left me a voicemail indicating she needed to talk about taxes, but when I got her on the phone I made sure to ask, "How's the wedding planning going for Natalie?" and we started talking about how that's been taking shape since the last time we spoke. Eventually, we got around to the tax stuff.

When you remember specifics, it makes the people in your life feel special. It's obvious that you listen to conversations close enough to remember them. That's big because we forget about 95% of the information we hear. The fact that you remember specifics shows you value people and relationships beyond the realm of business. Asking about the personal stuff first before you get around to business is a classic example of Meat Around the Bone Communication.

Sometimes these little personal touches might seem as though they shouldn't matter, but the truth is they do matter, *a lot.* Personal relationships are everything. My Meat Around the Bone Communication explains why so many of my clients followed me from PNC to my own firm. In fact, many of them were planning to be at my wedding before it was called off.

That's real depth.

Creating that level of depth takes time, but it's not exceptionally complicated. Little things like remembering what you talked about previously and being sure to ask the person about it really do go a long way.

One final element to add to this is that sometimes it's important to not only remember specifics in people's lives, but to go a step deeper and remember how they feel about whatever is happening. For instance, Laura told me recently that she got a new job. I've spoken with her a couple of times since then and asked her how the new job is going, and the last time we spoke she said she wasn't as busy as she'd hoped and she wasn't feeling sure about everything. Well, that's important information. Next time I talk to her I better mention not only the job but also her feelings about the job. I need to say, "Hey, is your level of activity picking up over there lately or are things about the same as they were last time we spoke? I've been thinking about you."

Some events are bound to be more meaningful than others. When you bring on a new client, immediately put their birthday, their spouse's birthday, and all of their kids' birthdays on your calendar. I have a specific birthday to-do on my calendar at the start of each month, and that's when I'll write out birthday cards for everybody in that month. I send them all on the same day, so everybody always gets their birthday cards ahead of their birthday. As soon as I'm done, I move that to-do to the next month right away.

Also, send handwritten holiday cards out. Find out which holidays are most important to each client, then set yourself calendar reminders accordingly.

Specific events, like an engagement, wedding, or retirement, should go on your calendar right away. Then call to congratulate people on top of sending a card, or a little gift. Calling is more personable, whether they answer or not. Leaving a message is crucial if they don't. It shows that you took time out of your day to give them a call.

I have a retired client here in Chicago, Marcy, who owns a home in San Francisco. For the last three years we've talked about how there's going to come a time in the future when she's going to sell the home. When she sells it, she's going to list the house for at least $2 million.

Well, that time finally came, and she got multiple offers above her asking price, which was great. But the first offer fell through. She went to the next person and closed for a great price, but it became a stressful period of time for Marcy. So once everything was completed and the money was wired into her investment account, Mike and I sent her a bottle of champagne with a card saying, "Congratulations, you sold the house! This stressful time is over. It's something we've been talking about for three years and it finally happened!"

That was a little something to follow back on, and we acknowledged her feelings about the occasion.

Another one of my clients, Natalie, has been with her boyfriend for the better part of a decade. They met in college and live together now in Chicago. They recently got engaged, which is *big news* because Vivian, her mom, would always talk to me about it. She was always wondering whether or not this guy was ever going to propose. And then it finally happened. It was big news.

I ended up sending Natalie and her fiancé some true love crystal Waterford flutes, with a note saying, "Congratulations on the engagement." And she really appreciated that.

These are little things, but over the years they add up. Calling people at the right time to say congratulations and sending little gifts really goes a long way. No advisor before me has done anything like that for them. So it almost feels like I'm part of the family. They were planning to come to my wedding when I was engaged. That's the level to which we've developed a relationship. It's beyond business. That's where following back helps you win more business, and Maintain Meat Around the Bone.

Be Someone Others Can Rely On

If you come home late, miss dinner, or brush off your kid's baseball game because an emergency happened at work, it diminishes your relationship. You can do it once in a while if you find ways to replenish the relationship in between. But if you're depleting your relationships habitually they aren't going to last long. Not eating protein for a week would cause your muscles to start wasting away. Relationships do the same thing.

You want to be building your relationships, not depleting them.

Put in effort to make people feel special. If you want others to stay in touch with you, you need to mirror that behavior back. It's the golden rule.

One of my clients is an extremely busy guy. Setting appointments with his assistant is almost impossible. I couldn't help but wonder how he and his wife schedule anything. Turns out, he has a separate Google calendar between him and his wife with all of the train schedules for his commute. She knows exactly what time he's going to be home each day based on what trains he takes. So while he's still very busy and might not be home at the same time every day, he makes an effort to be predictable and his wife can plan around it.

That's good communication. Set expectations ahead of time. Then follow through.

Follow up. Follow back. Follow through.

Every now and then, you'll get caught up unexpectedly and be home late. It happens. But that should *not* be routine. You need to strive to keep your promises. After work there might be an hour that you have blocked off to play with your kids. Fight for that time, even when you're tired. As soon as you let it slip once, you've opened the floodgates for your unconscious mind to make excuses every night moving forward. It gets easier to tell yourself you don't have to commit a *full* hour. The commitment, and therefore the relationship, starts to atrophy.

My friend RJ lives in California and he's somebody who I talk to maybe once or twice a year. But I reached out to him recently to wish him a happy birthday and we ended up talking. He mentioned he does a podcast on the side and he could bring me on to talk about my business. So we scheduled it. Except, then I had to reschedule it for the weekend. I figured I should *definitely* be able to do it then.

But the weekend came around and Samantha had to go out on a last minute commitment, so it was just me and Jayden. It didn't seem like a good idea to try and do a podcast for an hour while watching an 18-month-old kid. So I told RJ I would have to get back to him on a day that works. But I never got back to him.

To this day, I still have not gotten back to him.

That's a perfect example of me not following through. And has RJ reached back out to me since then to try and schedule it? Nope. He probably won't until I apologize and send him a time that works for sure.

As I write this, I'm making a promise to myself that I'm going to follow up with RJ and make the podcast happen. I'll report back on that in the next chapter. Still, the example begs the question…

Why don't I naturally follow up with RJ like I do with Francini? There's nothing superior or extraordinary that bonds me with Francini. It's all of the little things, every day, for years. You need to continue to nurture a relationship even once you've already won it.

In business, I've continued to nurture client relationships, take a sincere interest, and show honest appreciation. And it's paid off.

On the personal side, it's a work in progress.

Yesterday I was reviewing the accounts for Vivian. In general Vivian is low maintenance and never calls me panicking or requesting emergency changes. But as I was reviewing her asset allocations I realized a change can be made in her largest account that would benefit her from a tax perspective and help with her diversification by spreading out her risk.

So I called Viv and said, "Hey, how's everything going? How's Alex's restaurant with this pandemic going on? Is he doing curbside?" We caught up a bit and then I said, "Well, the reason I'm calling you is because I was just looking over your accounts and I wanted to run an idea by you. There's nothing wrong with the current strategy but we're going to make a few little tweaks. I wanted to gauge what you thought and then we can schedule another call with Alex."

That entire interaction wasn't needed. This was a client I didn't need to touch. I didn't have to look at her accounts. It's not somebody who I needed to call. But every now and then you have to go beyond what people expect. It Maintains Muscle Mass and demonstrates follow through on your end of the relationship.

My clients trust that I am acting in their best interests and informing them whenever changes need to occur. Because of this, my clients appreciate calls from me regarding their portfolio. It highlights my commitment to managing their accounts and it reinforces the trust they have in me. Whether I'm calling to make a little tweak in positions, completely reallocate their assets, or to simply gage their overall comfort and concerns with the current market climate they truly appreciate my calls. I need to get better about doing that in my personal life.

There are certain people who I fail to stay in touch with (like RJ). I eventually remember about them again when the next holiday rolls around and I find myself guiltily scrawling off a "Sorry I missed it..." card.

Relationships require constant touches in order to prosper. The people in your life need to be touched by you on a regular basis if you want to keep your relationships alive. The good news is it only takes a second to touch someone. This doesn't have to be something grand and dramatic.

There is nobody in my personal life who I follow up with in the same way I follow up with clients and potential clients in my business. There's Mike, who I talk to on a daily basis, and a couple other friends who text me nearly every other day. And Francini, of course. And that's about it.

I rarely follow up with my brother. I see my mom about once per month, but I'm sure if you asked her she'd say she wishes I called and stopped by a lot more often.

Much of the time, when I receive texts and emails during the day I don't see them right away because my notifications are turned off. I might glance at them during a break but I don't have time to respond right then. I get busy with everything going on and once I get home for the day I'm exhausted. I don't want to talk to anyone.

And that's a flaw.

With my dad, our calls happen automatically every week. But with other people, like my brother, the calls are rare. So I want to commit to starting a monthly call with him and working up from there, I am going to put it on my calendar and turn it into a hab-it. Think about your own personal relationships and remember you can adopt different strategies with different friends and family members.

Laura isn't someone I talk to on a daily basis, but we text each other here and there to check in. She'll text me during the day and I'll see it at the end of my night and get back to her within 24 hours. And that works for her.

Then there's somebody like my brother, who isn't going to reach out to me like Laura, and I'm not going to organically reach out to him either. So I need some kind of strategy to make sure I start following up with him more often. I need to actually put time on my calendar for giving him a call once a month.

Analyze your personal relationships. What is your starting point? What is a reasonable goal? You don't want to change everything all at once. You can't go from never talking to calling every day, that's weird. For my brother and I we're starting from not really speaking at all. If I can move to talking once a month and making sure I call him that's a huge step up. We can build from there.

Start where people are at and focus on making one change at a time, maintaining it, and following through on the goals of the relationship. I love my brother. I want our relationship to reflect that level of care.

How to make permanent changes in your behavior is the topic of Part 2. Most of the time we think of significant changes as being difficult and time consuming to carry out, but sometimes you can radically shift your behavior in an instant and never look back. That happens during moments of Recharacterization, and it's something you've certainly experienced before. In Chapter 4, you'll learn exactly how these moments come about and how you can manufacture more of them in your own life...

Part 2

/ Chapter 4
Recharacterization

Life's biggest changes often happen in an instant. When someone loses 50lbs, it's not the six months they spend working out that are significant, but the moment on Day 1 when they commit to living their life in a different way. The six months is the time it takes for their body to catch up with their mind. The real change happens in the blink of an eye.

Every dramatic shift in behavior starts with an equally large shift within. These instances of profound inner change are called *Moments of Recharacterization.* That's my term for something that causes you to shift your self-perception in a fundamental way.

These moments don't come along when you're calm and content. They arrive when you're at the end of your rope. Moments of

Recharacterization happen when your back is against the wall and you have no choice but to push off and come out swinging. They happen when you face off with your inner demons and win. They are emotional victories.

You don't lose 50lbs because you randomly decide, "Hey, it would be kind of cool to get in shape." Rather, this type of significant weight loss happens when you get so fed up with being unhealthy that you make a promise to yourself to get fit and never be out of shape again. It happens when you hit an all-time low and feel so disgusted with yourself that you're finally ready to change.

That's a Moment of Recharacterization.

When I moved out of my condo into a shitty 300 square foot apartment early 2018, I was at the low point of my life. I was suffering from a broken heart and engagement. Debt from the fallout and the move was drowning me. I had concerns regarding my position at the bank. And before the year was out I received the news that I was going to have a son.

I felt backed into a corner. I was pressed up against the wall with nowhere to run. My only option was to dig deep and come out swinging. There are two main emotions that can precipitate a Moment of Recharacterization: desperation and inspiration. Both have played out in my life at different times.

How I Got Desperate

I was in a sales slump and I couldn't seem to break out of it. My numbers had gone down every week for the past six weeks and that meant my pay was at an all time low. The job was commission only and there was no base pay, so it was painfully obvious when my numbers went down because I'd get a smaller check in the mail. I'd been in slumps before, but this was my worst performance ever.

My roommate at the time, Shaun, worked for the same company as me, American Income Life, and was also in a slump. Nothing seemed to be going our way. With our income dwindling and rent still due each month, it got to the point where we could only afford to eat once per day. Say hello to the McDonald's dollar menu. We'd walk in with a total of five bucks to spend between both of us, including tax, and we made it work somehow.

We both basically gave up on life. We lost motivation, and our sales continued to plummet as a result.

My boss, Matt, started bringing me into his office every day to role play sales meetings. He would pose as a customer and I would pose as the sales rep and we would videotape the entire interaction. Then we would review the videotape together and he would point out my posture, my tone of voice, what I was doing with my hands, my facial expressions…everything. Did I skip any sections of the script? Did I miss any clues about the customer's fears or motivations?

I always left these sessions with a list of ways to improve, but my performance wasn't getting better. After more than a month of this, I was nearing a breaking point. Shaun and I were still getting by on only $5 a day to feed us both. My health was deteriorating. I was feeling stressed and burned out. It was time for a change.

I tried to get a job at Ameriprise Financial to be a financial advisor. I got called back for a second interview. Then I got called again for a third interview. Then the regional manager wanted to meet with me personally. I showed up, excited and nervous. The manager was a great guy and we had a nice talk. But then he told me he wasn't going to hire me.

"I promised myself I wouldn't hire another kid without a college degree," he told me. "Every college student I've ever hired has dropped out because it requires about 60 hours per week to be successful here. And in order to become a Branch Manager or move into management, you can't do that without a bachelor's degree. So you end up getting stuck."

This was a Moment of Recharacterization that came from desperation. At that moment I realized I needed to go back to school. I stopped applying for jobs and started applying to get a degree in business. Six months later I was studying business at Roosevelt

University.

Desperation forced me to make a significant change. But years later it would be inspiration that kept me on the right path.

Getting Inspired In My Life

On Christmas Day, 2018, Jayden had recently been born. I was at my aunt Chrissy's house and my mom wanted me to share the news about my probable job promotion. PNC was asking me to move into a big leadership role and they were sponsoring me for the Series 24 license, which enables me to supervise and manage other financial advisors.

But there was an important caveat. If I chose to move into this role, I would no longer be a financial advisor. I would be managing other advisors. So my book of business that I'd been building for six years would disappear. I would have to hire another advisor to fill my spot and take over my clients. That meant I wouldn't ever be able to leave and start my own firm, because I wouldn't have my own clients anymore.

I was debating what to do because PNC is a great bank and I enjoyed working there. I appreciated my boss, Adam, and the promotion they were offering me was very generous. But I knew if I took the job I would be committing to PNC for the long run.

That's not necessarily a bad thing, but I'd be giving up my dream of starting my own firm.

After I made a small announcement about what was happening to my family, my mom said, "I'm not surprised they asked you to take on this leadership role. You'll do really well in that role. Just make sure it's what you really want to do and it's the best decision for you."

Her words stuck with me. I thought about it, and I decided to go independent. I attribute that 100% to my mom because her words that day were the deciding factor for me to go start my own firm. She inspired me to be true to what I believed I was capable of, and not settle for something conventional. I could always get another job if the firm failed, but I wouldn't always have a chance to start my own firm.

It was another Moment of Recharacterization.

Make the Change Visible

We all have many Moments of Recharacterization throughout our lives. Some are large while others are small. Maybe reading this book will trigger a small moment like this for you, a commitment to communicate with Meat Around the Bone more often. But how can you make sure it's a lasting recharacterization, and not a temporary one?

You could use a trick like the one Michael Jordan used.

The young college ballplayer, who went by Mike Jordan at the time, decided he wanted to be the kind of guy who takes the shot when it counts, not the one who passes the ball. He recharacterized himself. The next step was to ensure he followed through on this commitment. In order to hold himself to it, he did something visual and permanent: he changed his name. He translated his promise into something real that would remind him what to do when it counted.

Translate your goals into more than ideas. Look for ways to take internal commitments and make them external promises. You are always going to be tested. Change is never as straightforward as it sounds. You need accountability to motivate you to overcome obstacles, even the small ones. If you physicalize your promise so that it stares you in the face every day you'll be less likely to quit when things get hard.

Whatever change you're trying to make you need to write it down and physicalize it. Make it more real than any other idea in your head. I changed the name on my business cards because I see them every day, sitting on my desk. That was my way to physicalize my promise to communicate with Meat Around the Bone.

Physicalizing your Moment of Recharacterization could be as

simple as making a note in your phone saying 'Meat Around the Bone.' It might be a background on your laptop that reminds you of your promise to communicate on an emotional level, not just a factual level. Maybe it's something you've posted on your refrigerator that says "Don't forget the meat." Somehow your Moment of Recharacterization should be translated from your mind into something physical so it can remind you every day.

The most effective way to solidify your recharacterization is to tell other people about it. Make your promises public. Other people have an uncanny power to hold us accountable to our word. They often don't even have to say anything to keep you in line. Knowing you'll have to face one of your friends or family members and tell them you slipped from your promise is enough to keep you on track.

For most of us, the natural impulse is to keep our Moments of Recharacterization a secret. Often, we don't want to tell others about our commitments because we're embarrassed that we are in need of change in the first place. We don't want to admit we have a problem. It's also scary because promises mean we might fail and let others down. If you make a promise to yourself and fail, you only let yourself down. But if you verbalize the promise to someone else, failure gets even more painful. Fear of failure is motivating.

Another reason it's helpful to talk about your recharacterization with others is because they can help you measure your change and note when you're improving.

Yes, it might be easier and feel less vulnerable to start making the changes in your life without telling anybody or making a big deal about the 'new you.' Plus, it's much safer that way because you can always tell yourself you're trying harder and doing better if the only judge of your progress is yourself. Resist this temptation. Risk making your promises public. Once you tell the other people in your life about the changes you're making, they will start to monitor you and let you know when you're slipping. That can be hard to hear, but this bodes well with a business concept called "Pearson's Law."

Pearson's Law states:

> *"When performance is measured, performance improves. When performance is measured and reported back, the rate of improvement accelerates."*

If you tell your friends you're getting healthy and you're going to eat a salad for lunch every day from now on, that's a clear promise. They will hold you accountable. They might tease, "How was your lunch salad today?" or "What's for lunch today?" More importantly, they will observe your level of commitment. Even before you lose a single pound, the people in your life will notice you've gone through a change and they will start to see you differently. They'll stop inviting you out for burgers, and opt for a sandwich place instead where you can get a salad. When they see you're committed, their teasing will turn to support and encouragement.

When you order a salad for dinner, they might start making comments, like "Woah, two salads in one day? You're on fire!" When you skip happy hour after work on Friday to hit the gym, they won't give you a hard time. In fact, they might affirm you with words like, "That's awesome to see you taking this so seriously."

We humans are very good at observing patterns, especially when we know what to look for. It's like when one of your friends gets a breed of dog you've never heard of before, and then all of a sudden you start noticing those dogs all over the place. It turns out there are other people on your block with the same kind of dog, and you didn't notice before because you weren't looking for them. I've had this experience with cars, clothes, and electronic devices too. One of my friends got new shoes and wouldn't stop talking about them. Sure enough, I observed at least a dozen people wearing the same style the next day. These shoes didn't suddenly appear. I started noticing them because I was trained to look for them.

Similarly, when you publicize the changes you are making, people will start to notice all of your little adjustments that are consistent with that new change. I saw an interview with Mark Goulston, the author of the #1 book on listening, *Just Listen*, and he suggested that when you want to change a relationship you must 'create a wedge' between your past behavior and future be-havior. You need to make it very obvious to other people that a change has already taken place inside. Then they will start to no-tice all of the changes you're making on the outside.

On the other hand, if you keep your new commitment a se-cret, people in your life won't notice your efforts because they won't know what to look for. Your new behaviors will be like the dog breed and style of shoes before I learned about them. Your friends and family members have a fixed perception of who you are. Unless you make it obvious that you're trying to do things differently, nobody will notice your efforts.

Putting a wedge between your past and future behavior can be as simple as telling someone, "Hey, I could use your help. I'm trying to work on not making people feel stupid so you'll probably notice me taking long pauses during conversations to think about my responses and calm myself down. Please support me in this and also let me know any time I do something that makes you feel stupid."

This will not only serve to make others aware of your efforts, it will also bring out the best in you. You'll be turning your friends and family members into coaches who can hold you accountable. Just as athletes work harder in training when their coach is watching, you'll go the extra mile when you know the people in your life are holding you accountable to specific behavioral growth.

You need accountability to make the big changes in your life permanent. Don't try to do it all on your own. There's no shame in seeking help.

Mike Jordan became Michael Jordan by practicing and shooting more than anyone else on the team at all hours of the day, before and after the game. He became a legend because of his repetition, his routine, his work ethic, and his constant progress. And yet, he *still* doesn't make every single shot.

Even the best of us mess up and fail at times to keep our promises. We're humans, and we can't be perfect no matter how desperate or inspired we are. What separates the best from the rest is that the best realize their errors quickly and change course. The best aren't ashamed to own up to their shortcomings.

That type of dedication comes from a Moment of Recharacterization. Before making a profound change in your behavior you need a clear moment that prompts it. True change comes when your back is against the wall and you decide you're not going to give up, but give it everything you've got and come out swinging. Don't dread those moments. Prepare for them, and be ready to dig deep and make a decision that prompts a Moment of Recharacterization.

A Moment of Recharacterization can be a positive, defining moment in your life, but it isn't the only way to make a powerful commitment to change.

You Need To Break To Be Rebuilt

Recharacterization isn't the only way to make changes in your life. Small and gradual changes work too, especially if you have a particular talent. Pre-existing skill sets can work as a foundation for further change. For instance, after working with a health coach to hone in my diet, develop a morning routine, and dial in my exercise regimen, I don't need a recharacterization to force additional changes pertaining to my health.

I might read an article tomorrow about the magic of kettlebell workouts, or the awesome benefits of kale smoothies, and I'll start experimenting with adding those things to my routine. If they improve my life, I'll keep them. If not, I'll try something else. The commitment to improving my health remains the same.

A recharacterization isn't required because these changes are consistent with my view of myself as a healthy individual devoted to improving my habits. For me, adding kale smoothies to my diet would be a surface change, not a deep change. I don't need to reach another low point to start making kale smoothies. I need to get a blender.

Similarly, if you already have great communication skills throughout your personal and professional life, you don't need a dramatic Moment of Recharacterization like the one I had in my shitty 300 square foot apartment. Maybe all you need is to start experimenting. Take the tips in this book that align with prior commitments to change, and see what the benefits are. If they accelerate your desired growth, you will ensure they become habits.

These can be small changes. But they have to build on a previous Moment of Recharacterization.

Remember, profound and lasting change requires a moment that forces you up against a wall.

Sometimes I imagine what my life would be like today if I was still at PNC. What if I never had that moment of self realization? What if Laurel and I didn't break up? I wouldn't be at the point of writing this book right now. Nowhere close. I would still be the person I was when I worked at PNC. My health would still be in a shitty place and I would be treating people in my personal life with poor communication, taking them for granted.

My moment of self realization was what paved the way for my Moment of Recharacterization. Two years of contemplation suddenly crystallized to the point where I decided my mistakes had gone on too long. I promised to myself that from that point on, I was going to be a different person. I was going to communicate in a new way.

Laurel and I breaking up was the beginning of my journey of self realization. That was the catalyst. We broke up and by the end of the week I had moved out of the condo and into that piece-of-shit apartment living out of boxes. I was broke, and I had the financial burden of having to pay for two places and a lot of credit card debt. Then I found out I was going to have a son at the end of the year.

I was backed up against the wall.

People Matter Most in the End

In the aftermath of breaking up I saw many of my other relationships also start to deteriorate. Only my closest friends showed unconditional love and support. It was eye opening for me because I've never understood the importance of true friendship until now. I was cold and disconnected from others, and they showed me unconditional love.

My friends followed through for me in a big way even at my lowest low.

Nobody likes change. But the only constant in life is change. Change happens, whether we like it or not. I didn't plan to have Jayden. He just happened. And without him I might still be working at PNC today.

Many people commit feebly to change, but their motivation is short-lived. They don't persist long enough for the change to become a habit.

If someone tries something new but they aren't getting instant reciprocation from their partner, they will quickly start to think, *fuck it, she doesn't care. I'm not going to keep doing this.* But really if they would have tried one, two, or three more times…

Success requires persistence. It's about consistently taking the actions that lead to success and resisting the ones that don't.

Change takes time. You need to hang in there and roll with the punches before you can expect to see results. Accountability is a great asset, but sometimes you need the breakdown to happen. Recharacterization might be the only way forward. When your back is against the wall is when permanent change happens.

Even with my experience with Meat Around the Bone Communication at work, applying these practices to my personal life has been a challenge, and I'm nowhere near perfect. A big part of my motivation for writing this book is to physicalize my commitment to myself to communicate better with the people who matter to me.

Working on this book has already started to cause shifts in my behavior, even though no one else knows the book exists yet. The fact that I'm working on it, with the knowledge that people will read it one day, is causing me to examine my behavior closely and make improvements. One example involves my friend, RJ, who invited me to appear on his podcast before I had to cancel at the last minute because I was watching Jayden. I promised I'd follow up on this story in Chapter 3.

Well, Friday evening after work I headed over to Samantha's to spend the weekend with her and Jayden. On the drive over I thought about how I handled the situation with RJ, and I realized I dropped the ball. When I cancelled our initial call I didn't immediately schedule a new time because I wasn't at the office and I didn't have my calendar in front of me. So I said, "I'll get back to you with a new time." Except I never did. I got busy, life got in the way, and I never responded to him with a new time for the podcast interview. That was a week ago.

During my drive on Friday I realized that until I get back to him to say, "Hey, Saturday at 10am works fantastic," he's going to feel ignored. He's going to feel like he's not a priority to me. Really, I couldn't find 30 seconds during my week to put a time on the calendar? I need to get back to him to show that I'm putting as much effort into the relationship as he is. Otherwise it starts to feel one-sided. And nobody likes to be in one-sided relationships.

In retrospect, instead of telling RJ, "I'll get back to you with a new time," when I had to cancel the podcast I could have put something on my calendar and then changed it later. Or I could have set a reminder for myself and told him I would get back to him on a certain day by a certain time. Then at least he would have known I didn't completely ignore him or brush him off.

On Friday evening as I pulled up to Samantha's house, I sat in the driveway thinking about the RJ situation. It nagged at me. So before I left my car I shot RJ a text saying, "Hey, sorry I haven't gotten back to you. I haven't forgotten about you. That's completely my bad and on me. I will make it a point to look at my calendar this weekend for next week and schedule the podcast." And he said, "No worries, just put it on my calendar." And he shot me a calendar link right away. We got the podcast recording scheduled. Boom.

The Hardest Two Years of My Life

Deep recharacterization happens when you get to the end of your rope, stop resisting the need to change, and receive what the universe is trying to tell you. It happens when you are backed up against the wall. My wall was my shitty north Chicago apartment. If I was going to start swinging and fight my way out of there, I first had to reckon with the circumstances that landed me there. I had to acknowledge my mistakes.

That moment kicked off a two year period of self reflection that is culminating in the writing of this book. I'm putting everything on paper to get it out of my head and make it real. I want to hold myself accountable to my new commitments. After you make a decision to recharacterize yourself, the work is not done forever. It needs to be constantly reexamined.

Your brand is your first impression. It's how people remember you. How do you speak? How do you carry yourself? What do you stand for? Many clients have explained that they referred others to me because they know I can be trusted to hold high level conversations. My clients have already experienced similar conversations with me themselves. They know how I talk, and how I elaborate when asking certain questions. That positive behavior is so consistent that my clients assume the same pattern of behavior will be extended to whomever they refer to me.

I am now in the process of decompartmentalizing this brand. I'm trying to merge my professional brand with my personal brand so I can be the same person in all contexts. On the personal side I haven't been living up to the standards of my business brand. But after everything I've gone through these last two years, I've had a lot of time to reflect, and I know the change I need to make.

I need to rebrand myself. If I don't, I'm never going to grow to my full potential, and I may never win positive relationships in my personal life.

I don't want people to say, "Oh yeah, Jay can definitely help you with your financial planning needs, but he's kind of a shitty person. He brushes me off and seems irritated all the time. So I don't think I'll connect you guys."

If I want to continue to grow professionally, I have to grow personally.

My clients know they can approach me no matter what. And even if I can't solve their question immediately, I will make sure to find an answer for them or get the change made. The same should be true personally. I want my friends and family to know I'm their guy, but my behavior hasn't suggested as much.

The reason my breakdown led to a Moment of Recharacterization is because I am passionate about serving people and building relationships. I've always been a reliable banker. It was a huge wake up call to realize I wasn't reliable in my personal life. Weak personal relationships were the reason I was cornered. It was my desire to earn the brand of "Reliable Friend" that motivated me to stand up and fight.

Another good example of this is a story about a fellow banker named Katie, who works at a bank branch near me. Katie can answer my questions before I even ask them, and she puts Meat Around the Bone in all of her communication. She's a phenomenal sales person. But she wants nothing to do with sales whatsoever. She actually wants to go into operations and compliance.

I've told Katie she could be really successful and make more money in sales than operations, but sales isn't her passion, and so she remains stagnant.

The reason the turnover rate for sales jobs is comparatively high is because people tend to realize quickly that sales isn't for them. They're not passionate about it. Lack of passion is a common reason people quit when they are backed against a wall.

When you feel like quitting, it's a sign to either give up or double down your efforts.

Don't Give Your Power Away

Sometimes it's not you that needs to change, but other people. Cleanliness might be one of your strengths, but every time your friends come over they leave a huge mess and it makes your significant other feel like you're a slob. In this case, your friends are letting you down.

However, if it seems like other people are constantly letting you down, maybe you should stop and consider that it's not everyone else who needs to change, it's you. Stop putting yourself in a position where other people have the power to hurt you by making simple errors. You're giving your power away every time you do this. Humans make mistakes. That's life. But why would you consistently put yourself in situations where the mistakes of others hurt you?

You need to plan ahead and build redundancies into your life. If you are entering meetings unprepared, you should learn to schedule more preparation time earlier in the week. Don't be mad at your assistant for not being able to drop everything and help you scramble to get ready in the last 45 minutes. Be mad at yourself for not setting aside time to prepare. Adjust your approach next time around.

One place where I've had issues with this in business is when I'm waiting to get a response from a third party. For example, when one of my clients wants to purchase an annuity I will go through a third party company and negotiate rates to find the best deal for my client. Once I have a few top picks, these annuity companies will compile the information into a PDF with nice illustrations for me. I like to print these out and have them with me to show the client when we sit down to talk about the options. It's helpful to be able to hold something tangible.

I used to tell the annuity company to get me the PDF the night before my meeting so I would have a few minutes to print it out before the client arrived. But that strategy assumes the annuity company will get the information back when they said they would. That's not always a safe assumption. I can tell you firsthand that I look like an idiot when I sit down with my client and didn't have any packets to show them. The people from the annuity company don't deal with the fallout from that error, I do. I've learned to never be dependent on someone else to get me something without a large buffer period before the time I need it.

I now ask annuity companies to get me the PDFs at least a week before my meeting with the client, giving me plenty of time to find a different rep, or even an entirely different provider, if they are delinquent.

In business it's always good to have time on your side. Time is money. And money is power.

I saw many advisors when I worked at PNC who would fall into the trap of giving their power away. They would ask their assistant to prepare something only to be furious when it wasn't supplied immediately, saying things like, "You made me look like a total moron in there!" Of course, these individuals made themselves look like morons. They made the mistake of relying on someone else to do something that they were personally on the line for, without leaving a healthy buffer. That is never a good idea.

Holding onto your power boils down to being efficient with your time. Don't leave things to the last minute in any capacity, ever. If you want to be the type of person who makes sure nothing ever falls through the cracks, you have to build redundancies into everything. Provide buffers for the people around you to be human and make mistakes without ruining your day.

Now some bad news. After you go through a Moment of Recharacterization you're going to be tested. Hard. You'll have to climb the mountain to maintain your commitment to your new self. Circumstances are going to get worse before they get better. Do you have the passion, commitment, and accountability to roll with the punches?

Chapter 5
Roll with the Punches

In the 1997 NBA finals Michael Jordan and the Bulls played against the Utah Jazz. Right before Game 5, in Utah, Jordan got food poisoning. He was *miserable* and it seemed impossible he would play at all. But he ended up playing nearly the entire game and scoring 37 points and the Bulls won. He carried the team. This is an example of having your back against the wall, and having what it takes to come out swinging and make it to the next game.

Not everybody has that.

This chapter is about the aftermath of a Moment of Recharacterization. Once you've chosen a new brand for your life it's not easy to stick with it. The promises you make to yourself are going to be tested, and success may require superhuman persistence.

The silver lining? Once you get past the hardest part, things will calm down again.

Tough situations never last long. Tough people do.

It's like a boxing match; the scorecard resets at the end of each round. All you have to do during a fight, no matter how bad things get, is make it to the next round. You have to hold on and roll with the punches until the bell rings and the round is over. You don't have to hold out forever. Rest is only a few seconds away.

Everything In My Life Collides

The biggest Moment of Recharacterization I've had in my life happened the night I moved out of the condo I owned with Laurel and into a 300 square foot piece-of-shit apartment. That's when I vowed to change my communication and the quality of my relationships. But that internal decision didn't suddenly fix my broken engagement or my finances.

We ended up selling the condo at a loss, just to get rid of it. There were additional costs involved with the sale, and I covered everything. My back was against the wall. I had to pay for the condo, my living expenses, my credit card debt, and the engagement ring I'd bought (which was not cheap). Plus I needed to start saving money for Jayden, who was due at the end of the year.

I considered filing for bankruptcy, but that's a bad move as a financial advisor. So I decided to come out swinging with a passion. I wanted to be a person who pays his debts. I doubled down my efforts and attacked my job as hard as I could.

The rebound was significant and 2018 ended up being my best year as a financial advisor at PNC. I paid down my debts. First I knocked out all my credit cards, then I paid off the ring, and finally I settled up the condo.

I kept my head down and ground away, motivated to become the person I needed to be. When the end of the year employee awards ceremony rolled around I was in for a surprise. It turns out I won the Financial Planning Award that year. And the Insurance Award. And even the Market Leader Award.

Then the CEO came out to announce the grand prize, PNCs highest honor: the 2018 Market All Star Award.

"The winner is…" he said, fumbling with the envelope, "Jay R. Pocius!" The place erupted and I came up to collect my trophy. I was on top of the world.

At the end of the evening my boss' boss came up to me and told me he wanted to move me into a leadership role. He was offering me my boss Adam's job, which meant I was going to be managing all the advisors in the Chicago/Wisconsin region.

In order to move into that role I would need a specific FINRA (investment) license, and you cannot get that license unless your company sponsors you. PNC was offering to sponsor me. I knew if I was eventually going to start my own firm I would need this license anyway. I had to say yes. I was overwhelmed with emotion, but I couldn't quit. The real reward was still for the taking. I needed to come out swinging and fight to survive.

Give It Time, But Be Relentless

Real change is not going to happen overnight. You might have your back against the wall for a year, like I did after Laurel and I broke up. I lived out of boxes in my piece-of-shit apartment for a full year. I learned that your back can be against the wall for a long time. For all of 2018 my back was against the wall, but I was pushing off, stepping forward, and punching, hard. I would feel strong, like I was ready to step away from the wall. But then I would hear a song on the radio and suddenly think about Laurel, and the time we saw Taylor Swift in concert together. And it would trigger a flood of emotions for the rest of the day.

My heart was heavy and I still felt an emotional weight on me.

I see the relationships I've destroyed these past two years. And that's not who I want to be moving forward. That's not who I want Jayden to have as a dad. That last thought gave me the strength to push through a dark period.

An Insulting Offer

We were furious as we walked out of Wells Fargo headquarters. It didn't make sense. They had flown us all the way down to St. Louis for the week, put us up at their own expense, and they seemed very interested in doing business with us. But their offer was the lowest we'd received. It felt like a slap in the face.

There was added confusion to the situation because Mike and I were there as part of an event with hundreds of financial advisors from all over the country. We were the youngest advisors present by far. Everyone else was at least 50 years old and we were 30. We'd expected a great offer since we were starting J.M.Equity Advisors at such a young age and would have many more years to grow compared to the other advisors at the event.

Most banks will pledge money to your firm when you agree to partner with them. You can use the cash to cover upfront expenses like office space, computers, and IT equipment. When you choose to work with a specific financial institution that means you'll be clearing all of your trades through them. So the bigger your business gets the more money they make.

After Wells Fargo gave us their offer on our last day in St. Louis, Mike and I were pissed off. We felt they were shortchanging us. I got a call from the recruiter at Wells Fargo the next day and she wanted to know what I thought. So I told her that, frankly, I felt insulted.

"Compared to the offers we received from other banks this is a joke," I said. "And if this is what it's going to be like to work with you, we want nothing to do with you guys."

Over the weekend, she was emailing me and asking questions about what we wanted. I asked them to double their offer, increase the back-end bonus, and made a number of other requests. The reason I felt entitled to ask for so much was because we'd been the youngest people in that room. We were twenty years younger than everyone else and already at the point of launching our own business.

I told her to think about the future. With those fifty year-old guys there would only be so much time to get paid before they retired. But for Mike and I there are decades of business to look forward to. We are more valuable lifetime clients.

On Monday the head of Wells Fargo Financial Network (Wells Fargo's independent space division) called me and asked what we wanted.

And he gave it to us. He met every demand I made.

And from that moment we had 24 hours to think about it before the offer expired.

At that point I told Mike I was going to do it regardless of what he did. I was in. He said he needed to think about it overnight. And the next day he told me, "I'm all in," and we signed the commitment letter.

It all started with what my mom said that Christmas evening about who I am and how my dream has always been to start my own company. I did not want to let that go. I did not want to look back and *wish* I would have done it.

That Christmas inspiration focused me.

At that point in my career I'd received ultimatums from both PNC and from Wells Fargo. My choices were staying put and giving up my clients, or going out on my own and starting a business for myself.

Another concern I had was that PNC had sponsored me for the license. That means they paid for it (and it wasn't cheap). So if I didn't move into the role, that was money out of their pocket. I wasn't sure what their attitude would be about that. I also didn't know if I would ever have another opportunity for advancement like that again in the future. It might be my only shot.

I didn't know what they were going to think, but I felt backed against the wall again and I had to make a decision. No matter which way I went, I had to give something up.

I decided to take the license and run.

The deciding factor was what my mom said. I needed that inspiration for direction. When your back is to the wall, any decision to keep fighting is emotional. That emotion needs direction, and inspiration acts as the compass.

Coming Out Swinging

When Laurel and I broke up, things were complicated. We owned the condo together, which meant it needed to be split up. We had expenses and debt and at the same time my company was getting off the ground. I didn't know how I would dig myself out of this hole. How could I come out swinging from this wall? How could I make it to the next round?

It was the worst year of my life personally, and professionally it was the best year ever, in terms of money made and recognition received. I dug out of debt and continued onward. But something else was needed for me to reach the higher level goals of my commitment to be a new person.

When my mom triggered a moment of clarity and inspiration, she helped focus my efforts beyond the professional realm.

You Are More Resilient Than You Think

When you feel yourself breaking down from stress and pressure, it seems like your life will fall apart if you don't do something drastic to fix it. If you're not going to give up, this can catalyze a moment of self realization, and it has to do with understanding your resilience.

Resilience is the measure of your ability to keep swinging, even if your back remains pressed against the wall. Resilience accelerates recharacterization. The more progress you make, the faster you will continue to move towards your goal.

When my roommate and I were living on $5 per day and then Ameriprise told me they weren't hiring me, I didn't give up. I knew I needed to go back to school. It was a turning point for my growth. You can't always know the specific ways you are going to grow, but it's important to have a goal. Even if you're not moving straight towards it, you can tell if you're moving closer.

Ryan Serhant is one of the top real estate agents in New York City and the author of the book, *Sell it Like Serhant*. He spoke at a real estate convention and posted an 8-minute clip from the speech to his Instagram. I watched it 10 times in a row.

His words spoke to me. He started off saying, "Do you remember the moment when you first got into real estate? Because I do. It was 2008, the day the Dow dropped 800 points and Lehman Brothers filed for bankruptcy and the real estate market went to shit. That's when I started my real estate career."

Today, Ryan's one of the most successful people in real estate, managing a huge team in New York. That sounds like he's talking about one of those back-against-the-wall moments.

"Well guess what?" Serhant continued, "It's a completely new *decade*, not just a new year. It's a new decade. I want you to plan your goals and think about who you want to be and where you want to be not just for this year, but by the end of the decade. Because it's going to come in the blink of an eye."

He was talking about planning your life ten years in advance. After watching the clip 10 times in a row, I made Mike watch it too. Then I reposted it on LinkedIn.

Then I started taking Ryan's advice.

I asked myself, *Who have I become over the last 10 years?* My engagement fell apart and I made mistakes. How can I learn from those mistakes and plan to do better? There's a lot on the line now.

My conclusion? I need to let go of who I was during the past decade so I can become who I want to be for the next decade.

That's when I started thinking about what I wanted to accomplish and who I wanted to be. That's where the idea for this book came from.

You will experience adversity. What matters is what you do to keep moving forward. Resilience is constant reexamination, improvement, and change. The world changes all the time. What are you going to do about it?

Today, I don't do business behind any other firm's brand name on the door. It's my name on the door. It's Mike's name. The brand is who we are personally. They are inseparable. My clients know who Jayden is. At our client appreciation event last year, Samantha was there, my parents were there, and Mike's wife Elana and her parents were there. Our clients get to know us personally. They are investing their trust in us.

What we do as people impacts our business relationships. You never know who you're going to be introduced to or what new opportunity is going to come your way.

My own personal brand took a hit over the last couple years with everything that went on with me and Laurel. People on the outside looking in don't really know the details. Some have stopped talking to me altogether. Over the last two years I've thought about who I'm becoming personally and there are changes in direction I want to make.

Even though my personal brand has taken a beating, I can see the blow through a positive lens. It woke me up and forced me to look in the mirror and analyze myself: my individual traits (both good and bad), my insecurities, and my anxiety. This drastic blow has changed me for the better, because I've committed to myself, my family and friends, my business, and my son that I'm going to be a better person. I have grown in resilience and I will strive to continually analyze myself so I am growing in the right direction.

Once you make the decision to live differently, and roll with the punches to get through the hardest part of the change, it's time to start working on your routine. Adjusting your daily routine will support the way you live your life for the next 10 years. In the next chapter I'll show you how to do it.

Chapter 6

Change Your Routine

When you're trying to turn a temporary change into a lasting one, your routine is the most important place to start. Often, we set ourselves up to fail in our relationships because we adopt a routine that cripples our capacity to deal with certain people and situations. A routine that forces daily progress towards your goals will build your confidence. Confidence and positivity drive relationships forward. It's easy to feel upbeat in the morning when you are refreshed, but as the day drags on and the stressors add up, negativity can creep in and cloud your outlook. By the time the work day is over, you're ready to relax and unwind. Except, that's when your family and friends need you to be present for them. By letting yourself walk into the house depleted, or take your friend's call while you're distracted, you are neglecting your relationships. That's why a positive daily routine is integral to having strong relationships.

For two years I had been trying to eat healthy to improve my energy levels. I feel more energetic when I'm in optimal health. But I was struggling to get results. I was overworked and run down. Then I had a chance encounter that changed my life.

I shared a random Uber with a girl named Emily Golin, who turned out to be a private health coach. We got to work.

My initial goal was to improve my health. I wanted to be a morning person and have more energy throughout the day. I wanted to eat better. But I had some physical problems too, so that's where I decided to start. As we worked together and went deeper into my health she became more of a life coach. We eventually analyzed my job, my breakup, and my day-to-day rhythms.

In my line of work, January through April is always busy because it's tax season. During these months at PNC I had appointments scheduled from the moment the office opened at 9am to the minute it closed at 5pm. I wasn't eating breakfast or lunch because I didn't have time. I was running on adrenaline.

That's the state I was in when I started working with Emily.

I was constantly operating at a low level of stress. Every time I got an alert on my phone or an email pinged in, my stress level would spike because I felt like I was falling behind. When I got home I was emotionally drained from work. Laurel and I usually went out to eat or ordered something in, so we'd be sitting down eating a cheeseburger or some other fast food at 8pm, and that would be my only meal of the day.

I was exhausted. I was irritable. This was not a good mental or physical state, but I couldn't see how bad it was. Emily started by helping me eat better. We experimented with different foods to find out how my body reacted to each one. She told me everybody reacts differently to various proteins, fats, and carbohydrates.

As I followed her advice and experimented on myself, I learned there was a big difference between fish, red meat, and white meat. When I ate a piece of fish I felt better than when I ate a steak. That was something I'd never noticed about myself before. But it seemed obvious after Emily uncovered it. I feel energized and in the zone after eating fish. Whereas if I eat a steak I'll feel cloudy-headed.

Implementing A Morning Routine

The next step was to dial in my morning routine. Emily and I made different tweaks each week and observed how they made me feel. Nailing my routine was a lengthy process of trial and error. The key for me was discovering the importance of taking some silence right at the end of my morning routine. This gives me a chance to center myself and it also acts as a buffer between my personal and work lives.

Here's my current morning routine:

- Wake up and splash water on my face
- Brush my teeth and get dressed
- Drink my pre workout shake
- Hit the gym (and another 36 oz of water)
- Eat breakfast (typically overnight oats)
- Unplug for 10 to 15 minutes of silence
- Head to the office

At the gym my mind is all over the place. By that point I've already seen some emails come in and I've started thinking about the day and what I need to accomplish. 10-15 minutes of silence calms my mind. There's no right or wrong way to sit in silence, but guided meditation is a great starting point as you learn what works for your body.

With this morning routine in place I'm ready to take on my to-do list, which I prepared the day before and left at the office.

I have a plan and I'm ready to execute it. My mind's not going in a million different directions. I'm focused and ready for the next step. After that, it's time to put my suit on and tackle the day.

I never thought I could get by on less sleep, but with the right morning routine I've found five or six quality hours is all I need to feel energized in the morning.

A solid morning routine gets me in the habit of starting my day with positive thoughts and affirmations. That's the basis for a more positive attitude.

By the time I'm done brushing my teeth I'm *awake*. I might be sleepy when I first roll out of bed, but when I'm drinking my pre workout shake and heading to the gym I'm fired up. When I come home and sit in silence it's a necessary balance because my adrenaline is spiked from the gym. Without experimenting, and without Emily's help, I never would have unlocked this routine.

No business person should be waking up less than an hour before going into the office. That doesn't serve your day.

The right mindset starts the moment you get out of bed. Your morning routine sets the tone for everything you're going to do. It builds your confidence, and there's no stopping that kind of drive. It's completely different from waking up, hitting the snooze, rolling out of bed, and feeling tired on the way to work.

The Impact Was Instant

My morning routine changed everything for me. It empowered me to start eating healthier and to be more physically active. A well-formulated morning routine will make you feel good because you're eating and exercising in the way that works best for your body, and the daily rhythm of the routine will build your confidence.

I noticed the change in my mentality right away. The first time I ate fish instead of a burger, I felt great. I was doing it! The second and third times I felt even better. The way you eat impacts how you feel. It affects your body as well as your attitude. If your morning routine involves eating Jimmy Dean breakfast sandwiches every day before work, it might be affecting your mentality.

Try some yogurt and fruit. Baked yams. Sauteed kale. Poached egg.

Run some experiments for a week at a time and keep track of how you feel.

Emily walked me through it all. She had me describe my daily habits and what I typically ate. Then she suggested I test different proteins to see how my body felt after eating each of them. Every person's body has an optimal diet, I was astonished by how differently my changes made me feel. First, I altered my breakfast routine to the options of overnight oats or to two eggs. That felt very different.

Start experimenting with your morning routine and instantly feel the impact on your energy levels. I'm talking *immediately.*

Mindset Can Make Or Break Your Day

Imagine receiving a confrontational email. You could reply right away, while you're fired up, or you could wait until you calm down before penning your response. If you wait, you'll be in a better mindset to tackle the concern and put the appropriate Meat Around the Bone to bring ease and comfort to the exchange. The same goes for your mindset throughout the day. When your attitude is changing sporadically with your circumstances, you're operating at a constant disadvantage.

There's a difference between instantly replying to a harsh email and patiently responding. And there's a difference between instantly reacting to circumstances and calmly engaging.

Of course, every day is different. You can't follow an identical routine all day long without having to think through some choices. There's going to be some improvisation. But the way you *start* your day can stay consistent. That way no matter what gets added to your plate you're always ready for it. Even though circumstances will try to derail you, the right mindset can keep you on track.

Use a morning routine to take control of your day rather than allowing the day to take control of you. Unavoidably, confrontation will arise with your coworkers, boss, clients, spouse, and kids, but when you're in the right mindset, you'll be able to handle it calmly and patiently.

If you don't have a positive attitude, negativity will permeate your day and impact every activity you participate in. Your irritability will bleed into every conversation, presentation, project, and relationship in your life. You might think you're holding your emotions inside, but you're not. They're coming through.

I was not a morning person *whatsoever.* I never had been. My mornings were miserable. The first twenty minutes of every day used to feel, quite honestly, like pure torture. I'd always wanted to be a morning person and get my days going earlier, but I thought it was never going to happen. I figured I didn't have the right genes.

Today, however, I wake up early every morning. I swing by the gym and work out before most people even get out of bed. It fuels me for the day ahead. By 7am the hardest part of my day is over. It gives me confidence to accomplish all remaining tasks.

Read To Expand Your Mindset

I learned how to stop looking for problems and start looking for solutions. Today I assume I can figure things out. I developed much of that mindset by investing in real estate. It's not directly related to my career as a financial advisor, but it's part of my financial plan and it's important to me, so I've been reading a decent number of books about real estate investing. In that reading I learned a lot about attitude and how it affects all areas of life.

My point isn't that you should go invest in real estate, but you should be reading.

Reading is something I neglected for years because I didn't think it was relevant. I was too busy focusing on my career to read books. Getting into real estate was a blessing because it got me back into reading. And the knowledge I've picked up from books has enriched my life.

Audio books were a huge discovery for me because I hate sitting down to read a book, but I don't mind listening to it. Every book has something it can teach you, no matter what industry you're in. The question is whether you're going to read it.

You'll take away one or two really valuable things from every book. You'll learn a few nuggets that you can implement in your life right away. Changing my mindset was something I got from real estate books and it's been directly applicable to many aspects of my business and life.

As long as you're in the right mindset you're not going to have a problem taking control of your time. Remember, time is power. Being short on time is the lamest excuse you can give. Everybody has the same 24 hour period. It's a matter of how you use those 24 hours.

Constant Low-Level Stress

One day Emily asked me a question that threw me completely off guard.

"How about stress," she said, "what do you do to manage and cope with that?"

"I don't stress," I said. "I don't ever stress about anything. I've seen people who get stressed and that's not me."

"Everybody stresses." She told me. "Let's talk about your day."

I walked her through my typical day. She listened carefully. Then she said, "It sounds pretty busy. With all of that going on, what happens if there's an additional urgent situation and your inbox is buzzing with new mail?"

I scratched my head.

"How does that make you feel?" Emily asked.

"It bothers me," I said.

She asked me to explain the sequence of feelings I was having. Was it anger? Was it fear? Where did it live in my body? All at once I realized she was right: it was stress. I wasn't immune to it, but I was mislabeling it as anger.

"Ok, I guess I do feel stress," I admitted. "But I manage it well."

Emily smiled. "Let's find out."

We dove deep into my stress and we discovered I was operating every day under constant, low levels of stress. It was like a pot on a hot stove, boiling furiously beneath the lid. Without much provocation it could boil over. Little things could come along and trigger me to lose control.

Emily uncovered that notifications during the day were stressing me out. Each new notification that popped onto my phone added something more to my already overflowing plate, driving up my stress. The solution was a trick I stole from one of my friends. What I do now is disable all of my notifications on my phone besides CNBC and my work email. And I place my phone on *silent* mode. Vibrate isn't enough, I discovered, because when I hear it buzzing from a string of alerts it makes me feel like I'm falling behind.

So I turned all my alerts off. My phone is perpetually on silent now. Even when I do get a notification, like when a work email comes in, it only lights up. It doesn't vibrate.

It might not sound significant, but that one little switch has changed my life for the better. I can tackle my activities like my follow ups and cold calls and the phone stays silent. Sometimes I'll turn light music on for background noise because it gets me going when I'm talking on the phone. When I'm having great conversations with clients, my phone is face down. When I'm doing key business activities it doesn't matter who's emailing me. It doesn't matter who calls or texts me. I don't want to hear vibrations. I don't want calls to ring. I don't want added stress, so I don't invite it in.

I want to hear my music.

This allows me to focus on my calls to ensure I'm having positive conversations. I'm in a good mood. When I get a break I'll look at my phone and see who called and emailed.

The next key to staying positive with family and friends is to build a daily buffer to decompress between work time and personal time. Activities like working out, doing yoga, meditating, reading, listening to music, or going for a walk are all great things to do between work and home. This gives you a chance to calm down so that when you get home you're present for the evening with your family.

Maybe you don't have time to stop at the gym or do yoga after work. You can still do *something* to calm down on the way home. You can even sit in your car for 10-15 minutes before leaving the office, and listen to music while you take deep breaths.

One Of My Most Embarrassing Moments

From the moment a pot starts to boil over, when you first hear that ominous rattling sound, you have about 30 seconds to react or else you're going to have a hot mess on your hands. I'm kind of the same way. From the moment I first feel myself starting to boil over I have about 30 seconds to do something. If I fail to intervene during that window, it feels like I pass the point of no return and all hell breaks loose.

An example of this happened mid-2018. It was a few months after my big breakup with Laurel. Mike was getting married to his fiancé, Elana.

I had already started working with Emily by this point and I'd learned about my stress issues. I knew my emotions were bubbling under the lid, ready to boil over. And I was Mike's best man, right up front during the ceremony. As Elana and Mike were exchanging vows I felt my anxiety building up. I knew I only had thirty seconds to do something about it, but there was nothing I could do. I was standing in front of a room full of people. It got stronger. And I was trapped up there with everyone watching me and no escape.

The situation got so intense I passed out and nearly fell to the ground. The other groomsmen grabbed me and sat me down to catch my breath. Eventually I got back up and I was fine.

It was a case of anxiety coupled with drinking all day and not eating. To this day, Mike tells this story to our clients and it's become a laughing matter, but at the time I was mortified. The silver lining is that Mike's wedding was the last time I passed out from anxiety. It motivated me to work with Emily and develop more coping skills. I've become a morning person. I have a routine. I eat throughout the day so my metabolism is always working. I drink water throughout the day. I work out regularly.

I'm back to my natural weight, and I feel much better. Experiencing the impact of a healthier diet and exercise regimen is truly incredible. If you had told me before I experienced the benefits for myself, I would've laughed in your face. So trust me on this one. This morning routine was the key turning point for me. Of course, there are times when I still feel anxiety, but I can control it sooner before it negatively affects my day.

I 100% recommend anyone reading this book implement a morning routine – your own Miracle Morning. You will find, as I and countless other successful people have, by taking control of your morning you take control of your day. You take control of your life. If you're searching for help and motivation, you can also reach out to Emily Golin (www.emilygolin.com) or find another health coach near you. Coaches keep you accountable for making positive life changes. Once you've uncovered a better morning, and a better mindset, you'll find yourself leading a better life.

Everything Affects Everything Else

The wedding wasn't the first time I felt like passing out from stress. It's just that I'd always been able to do something about it before. During a few high stakes client meetings, for instance, I had to excuse myself from the room for a minute to breathe deeply and drink a glass of water. Then I brought water back for the client and made a comment about how hot it was, and nobody noticed.

Later I asked some of my colleagues present at those meetings and they told me I appeared completely normal. They thought I needed a drink.

Mindset + Attitude

The concepts of attitude and mindset fit together like a hand in glove. But they aren't the same thing. Your mindset is your internal ability to take control of your day, activities, and time. Your attitude is what you display to others. It's external. The two concepts complement each other but are distinct. It's good to own a positive mindset, "I'm ready to tackle this." When you couple that with the best possible attitude you'll be unstoppable.

You can do all the right activities and have a positive attitude, but if your mindset isn't there and you're still thinking about yesterday's problem or the fight you had with your spouse two days ago, you're not going to be effective. You don't want to be dismissive when you come home from work. You need to give close relationships close attention. You can take 10-15 minutes to decompress when you get home, but there are ways to settle down further in advance. I'll talk more about that in the next chapter.

The most pressing challenge is habit. If you've been communicating a certain way for a long time then people aren't used to you putting meat around the bone. This may be off putting to others at first if they are comfortable with the way you were communicating previously. It takes constant repetition to break down barriers to your future habit. It's going to take time for the other person to jump on board, and it's going to take a while for the new behaviors to become second nature to you. Stay the course.

I always believed relationships were important, but before I met Emily I lacked the energy to focus on relationships. At the end of the day, when I got in the cab to head home, I didn't even want to talk to the driver.

You get home, exhausted, and you have your family to deal with. Your partner is asking you how your day was.

It's *draining*.

You need time to decompress. Schedule it and make it happen so you can be fully present in your personal life, just as in business.

Missing Dinner On A Phone Call

In personal situations, the most basic way to follow through and keep your promises is to be home for dinner. If you're routinely caught up at work because you're not structuring your day efficiently with your goals in mind, that's going to have an impact on your family.

Learn from this recent mistake of mine. I was staying with Jayden and Samantha for a couple of months in the suburbs while I waited to move into my new loft. It was fun to spend some quality time with them and nice to enjoy some home cooked meals.

One night, Samantha was cooking dinner and it wasn't ready yet. A call buzzed into my phone, one I'd been waiting for all day. I popped into the other room to answer the call while she wrapped up the meal preparations.

I ended up being on that call for an hour. When I got off the phone, Samantha was rightly upset. I should have taken the call after dinner. I didn't know it was going to last an hour, but she had a valid point:

"You're always going to have clients. And you're always going to have to eat dinner. Find a way for these two realities to coexist in your life."

If you have problems being fully present with your family at the end of the day, add some time to decompress between work and home. It might be a matter of stopping at the gym, going for a run, meditating, or sitting in your car for 10-15 minutes with music or a podcast playing while you take a few deep breaths. Then be home for dinner.

Find a way to keep your promises.

We'll get into the nuts and bolts of how to actually do that in Part 3.

Part 3

Chapter 7
Systematic Follow-Up

In Part 1 of the book I introduced the topic of Meat Around the Bone Communication, showed you how to Fatten Up your relationships, and explained how to maintain your relationships to keep them strong. In Part 2 I talked about the difficulty of making significant changes in your life, how real shifts often happen in an instant, the importance of staying strong and rolling with the punches, and the power of routines to help you make changes permanent. In Part 3 I'm going to bring the information from Part 1 and Part 2 together and show you how to strategically implement the habits that lead to Meat Around the Bone Communication.

The idea here isn't to shift everything all at once, but to experiment with one change at a time. Watch carefully to see how each new habit affects you before modifying it or adding something new. This is important for many reasons. For one thing, people are used to you communicating a certain way. You can't change all at once. You don't want to shock everyone. Do it slowly and know it will take others a while to realize you're acting differently. Be patient and resilient.

You have to make Meat Around the Bone Communication a habit. This may be off putting to others at first if they are more comfortable in the way you were previously communicating. That's because it feels disingenuous for you to suddenly show so much concern. Expect that type of reaction. Don't let it deter you. Keep applying these tactics habitually and your relationships will start to change for the better.

To consistently communicate with Meat Around the Bone, the first set of habits you need in your routine is a system for following up with people about important events, questions, and information in their lives. It's important to follow a process that ensures everyone who contacts you receives a timely and complete response.

What's Your Onboarding Process?

In business, my regular follow-ups begin in earnest when someone becomes a client. I have a whole procedure for new clients to gather their financial information as well as their birthday, spouse's birthday, children's birthdays, anniversary, and favorite holidays. Create a system for meeting new people. How are you going to make sure their birthdays get in your calendar?

Have a way to make sure you will run your process consistently with each new person. I have signed up new clients and forgotten to add their birthdays in my calendar before. And sure enough the very next month it was their birthday and I didn't send a card out or wish them a happy birthday. That's why I developed an onboarding questionnaire. As soon as someone fills out their questionnaire, their birthdays and kids' birthdays are loaded into my calendar automatically.

If it's our first meeting we might not even talk about business at all. That's more of a time to ask each other questions. *Are you married? What's your spouse's name? Do you have kids? How old are they? What are their birthdays?*

This is not small talk. This is gathering foundational information to follow back on as you follow through with the new relationship.

I'm lucky in my business because most of the time somebody

will name their spouse as beneficiary and their kids as contingent beneficiaries when they set up their accounts. So I already need everyone's birthdays. If they don't name the children anywhere, I'll specifically ask, "Tell me, what are your kids' date of births?" Nobody ever hesitates with giving me that information whether I need it for their accounts or not. If you're not an advisor, you might have to get a bit more creative.

Be Nice... But Never Stop

Some prospects have told me they are busy running their own company and I can only call them on a certain day at a certain time.

When that happens, all I hear is: "You can call me." That is a green light.

Any time someone gives me a green light to call them I know that person is likely going to become a client because I have superb follow-up. I will follow up with a prospect every week for years until they either become a client or ask me to leave them alone. I've only had a few people ever ask me to stop calling.

If there's an opportunity, I will not stop.

That's what people want to see. They want to know I'm always going to follow up with them, be attentive to their needs, and push aggressively on their behalf.

There are many financial advisors who call a few times, don't get a reply, and give up. I read somewhere that the average sale happens after 5-12 touches. So instead of being afraid to follow up, expect it. Prepare for it. Welcome it. Following up is your chance to build touches until you get to 9.

"80% of sales require 5 follow-up calls after the initial meeting. 44% of sales reps give up after 1 follow-up." – Brian Williams, PhD

According to the Top Performance in Sales Prospecting research from the RAIN Group, it takes an average of 8 touches to get an initial meeting (or other conversion) with a new prospect. But the initial meeting is just the beginning. It takes a lot more to make the sale.

Use Several Forms of Follow-Up

I was stopped at a red light when a new text message came in: *Hey Jay, BIG deposit. Get back here now. - Norma.* I turned my car back toward the Lincoln Park branch and punched the gas. Norma winked at me as I stepped into the bank and she nodded toward a man in a dark blue suit sitting across the room speaking with David, a personal banker. I walked over to them.

"Hello sir," I said, sticking out my hand. "I'm Jay and I handle investment strategies for wealthy individuals here at PNC. Have you thought about adopting a passive tax-free income strategy to put your money to work for you and build low risk regular income?"

The man shook my hand and nodded. "I do think something like that might be right for me," he said thoughtfully. "I've just sold a house and I want to invest the profits well. But I also might want to buy another house. So for now I'd like to keep it liquid. Please give me a call to discuss this further."

He handed me his business card. *Lance Pratt*, it said.

"Sure, Lance," I smiled. Following up was one of my personal specialties. I had this guy right where I wanted him. "What day next week would be best to give you a call?"

"Monday," he replied.

"Great," I said. "What time works for you?"

"Nine in the morning," he said. "Looking forward to it."

"I'll talk to you then Lance," I told him.

On Monday I called Lance exactly at 9:00am, but got his voicemail. I left a message and followed up with an email. The next week I did the same thing. And again the week after that.

For months I called Lance every Monday, exactly at 9. A few times I called at 8:58, and he answered the phone, told me it wasn't nine yet, and hung up on me. When I called back two minutes later it went to voicemail.

During the entire nine months I spoke with Lance a grand total of four times. Twice he answered my 9am calls and asked a few questions. In both cases I promised to get him the answers by Thursday. When I called back on Thursday, though, he didn't answer. So I left a voicemail and followed up with an email.

Why did I contact Lance so relentlessly? Of course I wanted to win his business, but I also believe in the philosophy put forward in *The Million Dollar Financial Advisor* written by David J. Mullen, which says you have 12 months to turn a prospect into a client. If you cannot convert a prospect in twelve months, the lead is deemed cold and you should move on. I live by this rule and I will follow up relentlessly within those twelve months. When they don't answer right away, people are testing your commitment to them. They want to see how much you care.

Despite my failed attempts to reach Lance, I never gave up. I knew the opportunity was there. Lance expressed genuine interest during our initial meeting at the bank.

After nine months I was starting to wonder if maybe I was wasting my time following up with this guy. After all, I'd spent hours chasing him around and we'd only spoken a small handful of times. He'd mentioned a potential interest in investment opportunities, but hadn't made a concrete commitment to open a brokerage account with PNC—let alone to hire me as his advisor. It seemed I would be better off spending my Monday mornings prospecting new clients than following up with this lukewarm lead.

Until one morning I walked into my office to find a voicemail from Lance. He was ready to make an investment and was impressed with my follow-up. He wanted to give me his business.

Lance came in later that week and signed all the paperwork. He became my first million dollar client and is still a great client and friend to this day. Relentless follow-up won me a huge, lifelong account.

I never asked Lance why it took him so long to get back to me or why we only spoke on four different occasions. To me it didn't matter. He opened his account with me. I won his business and relationship. People will often find a reason to avoid meeting with you or taking your calls. You can't whine, complain, or give up. Persevere and make the prospect see why they should invest in you, or purchase a home with you, or trust you to consult and provide advice on their business.

One of the main tactics I used with Lance, in addition to relentless follow up, is I varied my communication strategies. I called, left a voicemail, and sent an email every Monday morning. This triple threat is very powerful.

When I started as a financial advisor for PNC, I stuck to one form of communication: the phone. Whenever I needed to follow up with customers I would call them and leave a voicemail if they didn't answer the phone. That was it.

But then there was a potential client who I spent months trying to contact. I followed up exhaustively without hearing anything back. I left multiple voicemails per week without any luck and then one day I thought, *why not try an email?* So I dashed off a quick message saying I'd been trying to connect with him for several months.

He emailed back within five minutes and said, "I know you've been calling me for several months now. I'm sorry, I've been very busy. There's no need to meet. I like you. Let's do this." We did everything via email. To this day I've never met the guy in person and have no idea what he looks like, but he's a huge client. We did eventually connect over the phone and handle all paperwork via FedEx. But his preferred method of contact is still email.

From that point forward I realized I was leaving money on the table if I didn't combine phone calls, voicemails, and emails together with other types of outreach in my follow-up. Now I also include handwritten cards in my communication with clients too.

I've found you can't possibly use too many different mediums to connect with someone.

I need to get better at using multiple forms of communication with the people in my family. If you asked my mom, she would probably tell you she wishes I called more often. I can definitely do a better job there. And I can start sending emails, cards, and text messages.

I'm going to start scheduling time on my calendar to connect with a few key members of my family on a regular basis, starting with once per month. Speaking of that, I have a calendar alert going off right now. It's time to go record that podcast episode I scheduled with RJ.

Remember the Little Things

After I started sending birthday cards to all of my clients and realized how much they loved it I've expanded that practice to my friends and family. I now put all my personal relationships into my calendar next to my business ones to send out birthday cards together. It's been a huge success.

Today it was Laura's birthday. I called her this morning and I'd already sent her a birthday card at the beginning of the month. It was great. Same thing with Francini. It's her birthday on Sunday. I sent her a birthday card. I'll text her on her birthday.

One thing I've noticed is, while the birthday and holiday cards are great, I haven't been reaching out to people randomly to just follow up. There are people who reach out to me and ask how life is going, how Jayden's doing, and what is happening with J.M.Equity Advisors, and I don't get back to them. I push it off and take forever to respond.

Sometimes it feels like there are too many people in life to keep track of. Remembering what you talked about with everyone sounds like a great idea, but it's not realistic. You participate in many conversations each day and discuss many different things. How can you keep it all straight?

For my business relationships I don't want to leave anything to chance, so I take notes after each call and I jot down questions I want to ask the client when I talk to them again. For Allison, an attorney who told me her brother was in the hospital with COVID, I wrote myself a note to follow up with her in three weeks and ask about her brother.

One of my new clients, Andy, owns a bar in Logan Square, a neighborhood here in Chicago. He doesn't have outdoor seating and he's been hit hard by COVID. He's still in a good financial position and he's doing some remodeling to take advantage of the time they are closed. When I wrote myself a note to follow up with Andy, I made sure to include, "Ask him how the remodel is going." That was all I needed to jog my memory so I could lead into the conversation with some concern and ask where he was at with the construction and whether he's opening his doors yet.

On the personal side it's trickier because I don't take notes on my calls with friends and family members. However, one simple thing I do is before I send a text or email to anyone in my personal life I will go back and re-read our prior communication up to that point. Often there is a long email thread or text message conversation that goes back in time. Before dashing off a reply, I go back through the last 5-10 messages we exchanged and refresh myself on everything we've been discussing. As I review I will generate a mental list of items to lead with when I compose my message.

Any time someone mentions something worth following up on, like, "My son is graduating from medical school on the 16th," list that as a to-do in your calendar. At the end of the day take a few minutes to think back over all of the conversations you had, and try to recall any mental notes you made to yourself about following up with people. Then I enter those into my calendar.

It's generally easier to execute these strategies when you are communicating with people over email or text messages because you can put reminders in your calendar immediately. During a face-to-face conversation it doesn't look smooth to pull out your phone and set a reminder to follow up on the 16th about medical school graduation.

Every smartphone has reminders. Anybody can set a reminder for an event that's supposed to happen or to follow back on something. It's easy to make sure everybody gets an annual holiday card.

How to Call People

I see a lot of novice sales people getting thrown off when a prospect doesn't answer the phone. What do people have against leaving a voicemail today? You can't get rattled by that. Leaving a voicemail is professional. Not everyone checks their missed calls at the office, so if you want them to know you called a voicemail is sometimes the only way.

Your voicemail can be quick. It doesn't have to be a six paragraph essay. Let them know you called, what time it was when you rang, and that you'll call back again later. Make sure to say your name clearly and a reason for your call that sounds interesting.

The second step is to follow up on the voicemail and send the person an email as well, letting them know you called and left a voicemail and will be calling back later. This email is often what gets a response from the individual rather than the phone calls.

But it's the combination of the tactics that works magic.

"Email is almost 40 times better at acquiring new customers than social media." – Brian Williams, PhD

It might sound simple, but this one-two punch renders a 50% response rate. The reason it works is because people don't like to fall behind on tasks or activities. When they see a missed call and voicemail, followed up by an email that says you've been trying to reach them, they feel the need to respond to put their own minds at ease. When they do respond, the door opens for a landslide of communication. If you are not utilizing this one-two punch, start immediately. Results will show up within hours.

Also, vary your timing. If you call someone on Monday one week and get no response, move that person to Tuesday next week. And if they don't answer a morning call, try them in the afternoon next time. Mix up your timing and approach to catch people when they are most available.

I can't tell you what kind of follow-up timing is going to work best in your industry and with your customers. That's something for you to figure out for yourself. Experiment. If you're always calling people at 9am-10am and not getting responses, mix it up. Try different strategies.

Don't Forget To Ask For Referrals

Referral cards are a pain to write by hand, but they have proven worthwhile. I ordered a box of referral cards on Amazon. They're like any greeting card. On the front, it says 'thank you.' And the inside is blank. I'll handwrite something like, "Thank you for your continued trust and relationship. I truly appreciate everything we have done over the last few years and I look forward to building our relationship and business together moving forward. The greatest compliment we can ever receive is a referral from you. So I've added three business cards for you to pass out to anybody who can benefit from a conversation." I send these out individually to everybody.

Asking for referrals is something you have to do, whether in person or via cards like me. It's an efficient way to grow your business. And in the eyes of the client it's another touch. I'm thanking them for their business. They don't have to pass out my cards. But it's still something they received in the mail. They feel special. I hand wrote it. I didn't have an assistant fill it out. It's something special.

I usually send out referral cards every quarter. At the end of December when I was visiting my dad, I brought out my box of cards and asked my dad to help me. His handwriting is *exactly* like mine. We each had to write 6 cards per day to finish the goal by the end of the trip. And we did it.

I sent those out to all of our clients, and from that effort we got three potential referrals. One was a very big referral. I use referrals to build up my pipeline of leads to Fatten Up my communication with. You have to constantly create lead flow.

Next, we'll look at my system for making sure you actually get everything done every day. Meat Around the Bone Communication doesn't work if it isn't steady and consistent. In the next chapter I'll show you the art of Time Blocking...

Chapter 8

Time Blocking

The art of setting aside time to complete critical activities every day is known as Time Blocking. It's about taking the tasks that are easy to delay and moving them up front and center. The process only includes three steps: deciding which activities to prioritize, scheduling your time blocks, and following your time blocks. However, this apparent simplicity is deceptive. There are subtleties to the skill, and challenges to overcome.

Prioritizing activities in your life is a broad topic, but it starts with a simple question: Which activities do you wish you'd been doing every day for the past two years? Start dedicating regular time to those activities. Maybe you'll think about where you would be in your life if you'd been reading every day. Perhaps it will occur to you that you'd be in phenomenal shape if you'd worked out daily for the past two years. You might realize how good your relationship with your spouse would be if you'd taken time every day to do something nice and spend quality time together.

The answer to that question is a great place to start when you're looking for activities to Time Block. Spend some time thinking about it and let your imagination go wild.

When it comes to your career, the most important activities to Time Block are the ones that grow your business. Those are the activities that will create a compound effect later on if you execute them consistently every day. If you can grow your business by a small percentage each month, or each week, then 10 years from now you'll look back and say, "My god, this thing is huge!" Look through your pipeline and make sure you're blocking in time for every step starting from acquiring new leads through closing a deal.

Many reps who are getting started in an industry spend too much time researching, reading, and planning and not nearly enough time taking action. However, life's most important lessons won't be learned until you get started and see what works for you in the real world. At some point you need to put the book down, stop researching, and start acting.

Never Be Overwhelmed Again

Unfinished business has a nasty way of following you around long after the work day is over. Emails and Slack notifications keep pinging into your phone. Your mind buzzes with to-do's you've got to wrap up before 8am the next day. You lack a sense of closure and completeness where you can relax and zone out. Time Blocking helps because it forces you to decide in advance how much time you're going to devote to each activity. Then, as long as you successfully spend that amount of time on it, you've completed your Time Block and you can move on.

Even when something you're working on takes longer than you anticipated there's no need to stress out. You can block more time tomorrow. Or you can email your team and inform them the task is taking longer than projected. The important thing is to hit your next Time Block. You don't have to get the project done, you just have to spend that much time on it. Pace yourself. There is a new time block coming up on your schedule, and it's time to move on.

When something takes a long time and spills into the next block, put it on pause and jump to the next thing. Don't feel bad. Don't worry. You did your part. If a certain task is always taking longer than you thought it would, some adjustments will need to be made. Jot down a note on your to-do list to figure out a new plan. Then move on to the next Time Block.

I hadn't figured out a system of Time Blocking when I got my first sales job selling whole-life life insurance. I was bored with the architecture program I was taking in college and I found a posting on Monster.com to sell life insurance. The job boasted financial freedom, a flexible work schedule, and a chance to become my own boss. I called the manager and scheduled an interview.

When I arrived, I found the conference room filled with nearly twenty people and we were all in for a marathon of interviews. The schedule included an informational video about the company (American Income Life), a one-on-one interview with the hiring manager, and a role play with a supervising agent. Anyone who made it past that point proceeded to an interview with the complex manager. I was the only one hired that day.

On its surface, my new job was simple: Each week I received a stack of forms filled out by new union members who had checked a box indicating they were interested in a free Accidental Death and Dismemberment Certificate. I was to call these people up, set appointments, deliver their certificates, and upsell them on buying a life insurance policy.

The job was 100% commission based. I wouldn't make *any money* if I couldn't sell. I committed to developing a thick skin, learning how to talk to people, getting over my fear of rejection, and mastering the art of managing my time.

At this company we had dedicated days in the office on Mondays and Thursdays. That's when we would make calls and set up appointments. Then we'd be in the field for a few days before coming back to the office, doing paperwork, and making calls to plan out the next few days.

During these office days they taught us to follow Time Blocks. Mornings were for paperwork and restocking our cars with supplies like insurance applications, oral swab tests, and accidental death and dismemberment certificates. The afternoons were for training and role playing. And the evenings were for calling new leads to set up appointments. On Mondays we would set up appointments for Tuesday and Wednesday. Then on Thursday we would set up appointments for Friday, Saturday, and Sunday. Then we'd repeat the process over again.

I loved the simplicity of this Time Blocked approach. It was effective and I've applied it with great success in many other areas of my life as well. After four months as an agent I was promoted to supervising agent and was responsible for training new agents. Every new hire started to spend time shadowing me and seeing how I set up my days following the company's Time Blocking system.

I didn't realize it at the time, but I was learning more than just a way to make sales. I was learning how to get tasks done without stress. In the years since then I've modified the approach, and today Time Blocking forms the basis of how I structure my days as I run a growing business. I've taught it to several other financial advisors, many of whom have told me they continue to use it with great success.

The Leads Dwindle...

My quick adoption of Time Blocking allowed me to put up impressive numbers from the start. I was chasing down leads, giving them their free certificates, delivering my pitch, and closing deals. Life was good. I was starting to think, *Hey this job isn't so hard. Maybe I'm pretty good at this sales thing.*

Except there was something I didn't quite understand about those magical lead cards that flooded my inbox every week. Those were filled out by new workers joining the union, and they were only sent to me if the workers checked the box asking for a free Death and Dismemberment Certificate. I quickly found out that after I met with a lead, whether I sold them insurance or not, that lead was done. And there are only so many new electricians, carpenters, plumbers, etc. joining the union each week. Pretty soon the leads dried up. The bundle of little cards in my inbox dwindled from 200 down to just 50. What could I do?

I learned how to ask for referrals.

I followed back with some old clients to see if anybody had friends or family members who could benefit from a free Death and Dismemberment Certificate. And I offered to give their friends the same deal, normally just for union members, since they were referred by a union member.

I also made cold calls. With my leads drying up and not enough referrals coming in to do steady relationship business, I got desperate. I walked around and knocked on doors. "Hey, I know this is random," I would say when people came to the door, "but I'm in the area and I'm giving free certificates out. Is this something you'd like to have a conversation about?" My sales picked back up. I received steady referrals, even from non-union members.

Adopting the right scheduling habits can yield massive benefits. But sometimes life throws you a curve.

During a business trip with Shaun (my roommate and co-worker at the time) I totaled my car. This left us with only Shaun's car between the two of us. Sales grew tough because working out efficient time blocks with one car for two schedules is difficult. Also, I wasn't able to have new agents shadow me anymore because the car wasn't mine. With only 1 car, our appointments were cut in half because only one person could commute to a lead's house at a time. Soon, Shaun and I were living on $5 a day and eating at McDonalds. That brought me to the point where the best use of my time was to go back to school.

Time Block Some Magic

Time Blocks can amplify your daily routine's workflow and productivity, and they can bring moments of magic into your personal life.

Laurel and I had a tradition where at the start of every year we would make lists of the best things to do in Chicago and choose our top 12. Then we'd schedule one each month. That was a form of Time Blocking. We were deciding in advance to spend certain blocks of time in a specific way in order to invest that time in our relationship.

What are some ways to Time Block magic into your life?

Maybe you've been thinking it would be fun to take a dance class, or an improv class, or go for a hike. Schedule it as something to do this month. Write it down with your family or significant other on your calendar. Maybe you can do it together outside of work and the other normal weekend stuff you usually do.

If you want to get another degree, but don't have the time or money to go back to school, try signing up for one credit at a time. It might take years longer, but that's not as long as indefinitely postponing your enrollment. When you use Time Blocks to prioritize your goals, magic happens.

Developing My Time Blocks

My Time Blocking approach evolved during my time at PNC Investments. The work ethic that helped me survive selling life insurance was helpful, but hustle alone isn't enough to succeed in the world of finance. At PNC I could only work banker's hours, 9:00am to 5:00pm. I couldn't outcompete everyone else based purely on volume alone. I needed to become more efficient with my time.

There were also considerably more responsibilities at PNC demanding my time. There were days when I had a *ton* of paperwork to do. There were days when I had to make mountains of follow-up calls. Half of each day was consumed by unnecessary conference calls. But at the end of the day it was my responsibility to ensure I was always, somehow, growing my book of business. If I spent my whole day doing administrative tasks or following up on to-do's with current clients, I wasn't growing my business. And if you're not growing in the business world, you're dying.

My business development activities were my top priority, and

I needed to use Time Blocks to make sure I got them done. That was the key that caused my career to explode.

I still follow this key today and it's the biggest factor in my success, aside from Meat Around the Bone Communication. My Time Blocking schedule varies based on the day of the week, and I dedicate two or three days each week to being in the office with my business partner, Mike. That gives us time to tackle certain tasks together. On the other two days I work from home and focus on my individual clients, and Mike does the same.

When we're in the office together, our days look like this:

TIME	ACTIVITY
8:30am-9:30am	Follow-up calls with current clients and daily to-dos
9:30am-10:30am	Cold calling purchased lead lists or client referrals
10:30am-11:30am	LinkedIn prospecting and setting up referrals and interviews
12:30pm-2:30pm	Interviews and joint appointments with Mike
2:30pm-5:30pm	Preparing financial plans and presentations/additional interviews

As our company grows and evolves and the demands of our business change, my schedule of daily Time Blocks will change with it. But for now this is what I do. Instead of getting into the office whenever I feel like it, spending time chatting with Mike, or hanging around watching the market, I consciously prioritize the specific tasks that most effectively grow my business. From the moment I get into the office to the moment I leave I'm productive because I have a plan for what I'm going to do with every minute of the day before I start.

These blocks aren't random. They aren't chosen based on my chronotype or body morphology or anything fancy like that. I adapted this system based on what I've noticed works best for my clients and prospects. I've observed people are most likely to answer cold calls between 8:30am and 10:30am in the morning. So even though I'd rather make my calls at 2 in the afternoon, I schedule them starting at 8:30am. Similarly, my clients love getting calls first thing in the morning because it makes them feel important when I follow up with them about things right away. So 8:30am is when I block those calls in.

The goal is to make your time in the office as efficient as possible. Spend it on your highest priority activities. That means anything that grows your business.

Don't Be Afraid to Divide the Labor

When I was at PNC I had Francini, so I was able to rely on her for help. I could delegate tasks to her if they had to get done right away. But now with only me and Mike, we have to schedule our time efficiently because there's nobody to pick up the slack if we can't get everything done.

There have been times when I asked Mike for his help finishing a to-do because I needed to take care of something else. And vice-versa. So at least the two of us can help each other out. But that's our only line of defense, and we treat it as a last resort.

Obviously not every sales person has a partner or an assistant, especially early in your career. But it is okay to delegate where you can, as long as you're not abusing your power. Your job is to get the work done, not necessarily to do it all by yourself. Focus your time on things that grow the business and delegate tasks that don't lead to growth.

There are times when I'm looking at my schedule for the next day and I craft an email to Mike saying, "Hey, I'm going to need help on a few things tomorrow." If he has capacity he can help me accomplish anything I'm behind on that needs to get done right away. That kind of teamwork makes things easier for everyone.

Prioritize Business Development

My time blocks are specific to J.M.Equity Advisors. You'll need to decide for yourself which activities are important enough to include in your daily time blocks. Regardless of your industry, whether you're a real estate agent, pharmaceutical rep, or estate planning attorney, the first thing you need to do is think about activities that will grow your business. What are your core business development activities?

Generating new leads for your business is the #1 most important activity to perform regularly. Without a steady flow of leads everything else will grind to a halt. You need to complete lead generation activities to grow your business. If you're in sales (which most of us are in one form or another) there's often some form of cold calling or drop-by.

If you're a real estate agent, you probably spend time each day going through new local listings and calling the owner to say, "Hey, I saw your listing doing it all yourself. I would love to view your unit and see how I can potentially get you more money on your sale and learn why you priced it the way you did in your listing." For pharmaceutical reps there is a process of calling hospitals to get in front of doctors so you can teach them about better technology and new treatments. These cold outreach activities will generate more leads and gain you new clients.

Asher is a client of mine who sells industrial cleaning supplies to big pharma companies in the Midwest for maintaining their clean rooms, and he routinely calls up new companies before dropping by their headquarters to generate business.

If you can't think of ways to generate new leads in your business, consider one of the most basic approaches of all. There are companies that will sell you a list of contacts meeting certain criteria. For instance, I'm a financial advisor in Chicago so I might want a list of families with a household income above a certain level who purchased a home in the Lincoln Park neighborhood back in the 60s, 70's, or 80's. Today that brownstone is worth over a million dollars and they might be looking to downsize, invest the extra money, and prepare for retirement. I want to call those people up and introduce myself.

Another good place to look is at your competition. What are other people in your industry doing to generate new leads? Are there any strategies you can mirror from sales reps in similar industries? You can also block time for follow ups and other important activities that move prospects along your pipeline.

Get Your Schedules Coordinated

Even when Mike and I aren't in the office together, we follow the same daily schedule of Time Blocks. This makes it easy to help each other out as needed. If something urgent comes up and I need to ping Mike, I'm not going to interrupt him while he's making cold calls. I could send him a LinkedIn message at 10:30am when I know he's going to be logging into LinkedIn. Or I could drop him a note to call me during lunch.

Having dedicated times when we're doing predictable tasks helps us avoid stepping on each other's toes.

Time-blocked activities are permanently ingrained on the calendar. Some appointments change every day, though. On days when Mike and I are out in the field meeting with individual clients, we still use the same shared calendar. Anyone who joins our firm will be expected to do the same. Transparency is key to successful Time Blocking. I don't want Mike calling me when I'm meeting with a client to review their portfolio. Appointments need to be visible to Mike and my firm. Everyone can see my daily activities and when I have free time.

Not every day stays on schedule. Sometimes it's necessary to shuffle Time Blocks to make everything work. Mike and I share our calendars so we can always know what the other person is up to. That way if I see he has an hour blocked off for appointments or follow ups I know not to disturb him because I don't want to take his attention away from that activity.

Without this level of coordination, time gets wasted. Mike will call to ask me a question, or vice versa. Before I know it, ten or twenty minutes will have gone by, and that was time I had planned to spend growing my business. Time blocks must be kept sacred.

They are non-negotiable commitments once on your calendar. These activities *need* to happen in order for your business to grow and live on. You never want to be comfortable sitting in the office doing nothing.

It's rare to have something come up that is important enough to derail you from your Time Blocked activities. However, it can happen. There are emergencies that must be dealt with right away. In those situations where you end up missing some important business development time during the day, always find a way to make it up somehow. Even if Mike was able to complete his Time Blocks without me, that's not the same as both of us completing them. So I will usually go in and schedule some extra time for myself later in the week to compensate.

For most of us, interruptions are unavoidable. It's not realistic to think you can plan your day from A to Z and have everything go exactly according to plan, every time. If something urgent comes along and you need to tackle it, go for it and don't feel guilty. You have to take care of it and it's not something you could have planned for. But that doesn't mean the rest of your day is out the window. As soon as you finish up with whatever it is, pick right back up with your Time Blocks. Make a note of the blocks you skipped and add them to your calendar for later in the day or week.

Don't beat yourself up about things you can't control. But you also can't let that time go by and forget about making it up.

Everybody has busier days and slower days throughout the week. Missed Time Blocks happen, but they need to be made up somehow, whether it's by taking a working lunch, staying a bit later at the office, or waking up earlier and coming in the next morning to tie up loose ends before your first scheduled Time Block arrives at 8:30am and you start cold calling.

Also, if this is consistently happening, block in 30 minutes at the end of your day to catch up on things you fell behind on.

Blocking Personal Time

I started to wonder what would happen if I applied the Time Blocking approach to my personal relationships as well as my business ones. What if I devoted specific time each day and each week to Fattening Up and Maintaining Muscle Mass in my relationships with my family and friends?

You don't have to approach your personal life in such a systematic way like I do in the business world (and many people would say it defeats the entire point to do so), but Time Blocking is a huge secret to my success in business and I wondered whether it could be applied to the personal realm.

When you have your son's baseball game you're planning to attend, or a date with your spouse scheduled, put it in your work calendar and block it off. Allow everybody in your business to see it. The people you work with should know not to call you during your son's baseball game.

I've started blocking off my entire Friday afternoon and most of my weekend to spend time with Jayden. Everyone in my business knows not to expect anything from me during that time because I'm going to have my phone off (or on silent *at least*) and be devoted to my family. This wasn't the easiest practice to implement, as I have clients who prefer to meet on Saturdays due to work schedules. Before Jayden, I was able to meet with anyone over the weekend. Now I need to be more efficient with my time. Not only that, I need to be transparent about why I adjusted my schedule to take Friday afternoons and weekends off.

I've discovered my clients who once preferred to meet on Saturdays now enjoy keeping the weekends to themselves. Additionally, my clients know about Jayden and whole-heartedly expect me to spend Friday afternoon and weekends with him. This is never a concern for my clients and it makes us feel more connected.

The first step to improving anything is blocking off time to work on it. If you want to Fatten Up your personal relationships, or Maintain their Muscle Mass, you're going to have to block off time on a regular basis to work on it. Anybody can do that. But most of us don't.

Time Blocking Personal Calls

Tuesdays at noon I talk to my dad. It's been that way for over a decade and a half. The tradition started when I left home for college. I'm not exactly sure why we settled on Tuesdays at noon. That must have been when I had a lull in my classes or when my dad had a break in his work schedule. The talks were always casual. Nothing heavy, just checking in on life and keeping in touch.

Even after I graduated college, worked at PNC, and later started J.M.Equity Advisors, this tradition stuck. My class schedule didn't exist anymore, and my dad has retired from that job, but for some reason, Tuesdays at noon we talk.

These father-son chats are an example of Time Blocking important personal calls, and it's something I want to get better at doing with more people in my life. For instance, my brother and I don't connect nearly as frequently simply because we haven't made it a deliberate habit. I often think, *hey I should check up on him!* But then my mind goes to something else and I don't follow up. I never purposely block time to fully commit to connecting with him.

And that's something I'm realizing as I work on this book.

Share A Calendar With Your Family

Mike and his wife, Elana, have a specific Google calendar that they share. Working late? It's on the calendar. Volleyball practice? Check the calendar. Visiting with family? Calendar.

When I saw how well Mike's system works, I had a conversation with Samantha and explained how my mind is constantly going. I said, "If something needs my attention, or I need to stay an extra day in the city, or if the daycare is closed, or there's a doctor's appointment, send a calendar invite to my work email so I get it instantly. Then I can put it on my calendar and it will show up when I'm planning my week and looking ahead at the coming days.

That was a game changer because I'm *always* looking at my work calendar and email. Any time I get a notification, no matter what I'm doing, I see the email. So adding important personal events to that calendar was a revelation for us. It was a way for me to ensure I'm Maintaining Muscle Mass with my family. Now I never miss anything.

This chapter comes down to keeping your promises and doing what you say you're going to do. Put it in your calendar, Time Block it, and make sure it happens. Set up your calendar in the most efficient way possible. Make it easy for yourself to follow through.

Respond Quickly to "Emergencies"

Even with most of my weekend blocked off for Jayden, I've found there's still time to get back to people within 24 hours on anything important. Jayden is in bed by eight o'clock. If someone calls me Saturday afternoon I'm not going to answer. But if they leave me a voicemail I'll listen to it before bed and I can dash off a quick email letting the person know I got their message and I'm glad they contacted me, and I'll follow up with them first thing Monday morning.

Clients appreciate these quick responses. Especially since I've let them know I don't work on the weekends. Therefore they are even more grateful when I do take the time to let them know I saw their message and their request is on my radar.

Of course, you can never plan for *everything*. There are going to be times when events come up that require your attention, and you can't stick to your Time Blocks. Maybe you were planning to go camping this weekend with your family, but a pipe burst in your basement and now there's a huge flood. Camping has to be rescheduled.

Or maybe I'm reviewing a client's portfolio, but I see a message come through from Mike and the subject looks time sensitive. I might click over to the message and deal with it right away. It's difficult to focus on the task at hand when you've seen something big pop into your messages. That's why the best policy is usually to save yourself from the temptation. If you've got an hour blocked off for your daughter's music recital, turn off your phone during that time—or at least the notifications. Or maybe leave it hidden in the car.

Because whether you see the message immediately or an hour later isn't going to make a difference. But once you do see it you'll be distracted. Remove that problem and don't look at your phone when you've blocked off personal time on your calendar.

One Size Doesn't Fit Them All

With my mom, things are different than they are with my dad. For one thing, my mom and I live in the same city and we see each other once a month, while I only see my dad once or twice per year. So what's the right level of calls with her? And what's the best way to block those out? This is something I'm still working on. I find that in a given week I may speak to my mom a few times, or not at all. I should schedule a Time Blocked call with her. In fact,

I'm putting that on my to-do list right now…

There are other people you stay in touch with less frequently. These are people you consider friends or family but who aren't in your day-to-day life. Maybe they are family members such as aunts or uncles, or cousins that you see occasionally at family parties, events, and holidays. Or maybe they are friends from high school or college who you routinely stay in touch with. You don't want to connect with them every day or every week but you still want to check in periodically.

Jacob is a friend who I went to high school with and we don't stay in touch on a regular basis. But every couple months we touch base and call each other. Last year I took a trip to North Carolina, DC, and New York and I visited Jake in DC. That was fantastic. But he's not somebody I talk to on a daily basis or even a weekly basis.

After working on this book I've started to block out time once per month to go through and connect with those people who I want to stay in touch with but don't need to connect with every week. Not every person is going to get touched every month, but by scheduling the time I can at least make sure I'm conscious about spending time growing my relationships, same as my business.

Don't Block Out ALL Of Your Time

Of course, if you go too crazy with Time Blocking then pretty soon your whole day is blocked out and you don't have any time left for spontaneity. Time Blocking is powerful, but it's also resource intensive. It involves devoting continued effort to something over an extended period of time. In your business you have to prioritize top goals. In your personal life think of a handful of relationships to focus on. Set these as your current priorities.

But that doesn't mean you shouldn't put any effort into the relationships that don't make your list. I often find myself ignoring texts completely. I tell myself I'm going to get back to the person, but then I get busy and forget about it. Instead, I should have responded and said, "Hey, I can't talk right now but let me give you a call this weekend."

When you can't get back to someone immediately, add them to your to-do list. Either schedule a time in your calendar to give them a call, or set a to-do reminder to follow up with the person on a specific date. Various people will always ping you, and most won't be scheduled. It's important not to blow them off or forget about them. Acknowledge them, thank them for reaching out, and provide a time to touch base. Then add them into your to-do list, or Time Block them.

During my weekends I don't put anything on my calendar

from Friday afternoon throughout the end of Sunday night. That's my time with Jayden. When he goes down for a nap Sunday afternoon or after he goes home Sunday evening, that's when I pick up and make a quick plan for Monday. That's also when I'll get back to people I didn't get back to since Friday.

Spend a few minutes at the end of your day responding to unanswered emails and texts. Sometimes when you're having a busy week you might not get to that every day. There will be people you miss who need responses when you've been too swamped to reply. In those cases, set a reminder to get back to them on Saturday morning or Sunday evening.

If there is somebody you need to follow up with, like RJ for the podcast, set a reminder in your phone to make sure you follow up with them. That task will only take a couple minutes, so when the reminder comes in it's easy to take care of it.

Time Blocking is the biggest key to making sure you get back to everyone in a timely manner. Set aside time every day to follow up with people.

When I told my friend RJ I'd find a new time to record a podcast with him I set a reminder in my phone to make sure I reached out to him on Friday afternoon. When I arrived at Samantha's house I saw that reminder and, before I even got out of my car, I sent RJ a text saying, "Let's schedule this podcast." And we got it done right away.

Don't Let People Slip Through the Cracks

My problem is that I get busy and I forget somebody called me or texted me. So I never get back to them. Most people might give me the benefit of the doubt and think, *Jay cares but he's really busy.* But after that happens several times, they're never going to call me or check in with me again. That relationship has lost muscle mass.

Nobody wants to feel like they're a low priority.

Why would they keep checking in with you if you're never going to respond? It's one thing to tell people you're going to get back to them if you actually do it. It's another thing if you fail to follow up. If you actually reply on Sunday like you said you would, they are assured you do care. But if you don't respond, people feel they're a low priority.

For most of us, it's unrealistic to respond to everyone immediately. As long as you reply within 24 hours, you are covered. It might be as simple as reaching out to schedule another time to touch base. But don't ignore them.

Respond and acknowledge that you see the person reached out to you and promise to follow up. Then set a reminder to make sure it happens.

Getting Started with Time Blocking

The best way to get started with Time Blocking is to analyze the activities you generally engage in during a business day that are integral. Write them down. What are the activities you need to be doing every day to grow your business? Now organize them and structure them in a way you think will be more efficient than what you're doing now and execute it for the next week. At the end of the week, look back over your schedule and adjust it as you plan out the next week.

It takes some experimentation to arrive at the perfect balance of structure and freedom with your Time Blocks. I like to have about 5 blocks during my day, but some people prefer more blocks and others like to have fewer blocks that are longer in duration. The only way to find what works best for you and your business is to try as many things as possible. You never know if an activity might work better at a different time of day until you test it. The worst that will happen is you'll find out something doesn't work, which is helpful information to have.

This practice gets powerful for putting Meat Around the Bone when you combine it with your daily to-do list...

Chapter 9

Rethinking the 'To-Do' List

Most of the things you need to accomplish as you maintain Meat Around the Bone Communication are so quick they won't require their own Time Blocks. The majority of these tasks, like dashing off a Happy Birthday email, responding to a text message, or scheduling a follow-up call, can be taken care of in a minute or two. But if you interrupt whatever you're doing to address these as they come in you'll be repeatedly pulled away from your main task. That slows you down and kills your productivity and focus. The solution is to collect all of these smaller to-dos on a list as they come in. Then you can Time Block a chunk of time each day to address everything on your to-do list.

There are many ways to keep track of your to-do list. I've seen successful people use all types of methods from pads of paper to productivity apps to day planners to post-it notes to secretaries. The main requirement is that you need some place to capture tasks as they come in and organize them for easy completion later. Keep the list somewhere highly visible so it will constantly get your attention and remind you about your to-dos. I like to keep mine as an open window on my computer screen. Some people leave it on a whiteboard. Others put post-it notes on their wall. You *cannot* leave the office until you've listed out your to-do's for the next day. That's how I approach it.

There is no such thing as not having enough time. If that's how you feel, it means you need to think about how you structure your day and which activities you're Time Blocking. Even if I don't finish all of my to-do's in the hour from 8:30am to 9:30am, I know I'm going to have some time in the afternoon when I can work on the rest. Not every day is jam-packed with appointments and interviews. There's going to be time later on when you can get things done.

As you complete your to-do's, erase them, delete them, tear them off, or throw them away. You should see at a glance everything you still need to accomplish. Over the course of your day you should be checking off to-do's and adding new ones for the next day. Before you leave the office, organize your list for the following day and block some time on your calendar to complete it. Throughout the day you can always be preparing for the next day by saving your to-dos as they come in. This way at the end of the night when you're getting your to-do list ready for the next day you'll be much more efficient.

By the time I finish for the day and shut down my laptop, I have a full to-do list for the next day already saved on my calendar. Knowing that I already have my calendar set up and structured with Time Blocks makes me feel motivated.

You can also keep a separate list of people you're trying to get a hold of, divided into days of the week with a section for people you want to follow up with on Monday, another section for Tuesday, and so on. Put a daily Time Block on your calendar to reach out to everyone on your follow-up list with that triple threat of calling, leaving a voicemail, and sending an email. If you reached out to someone but weren't able to connect with them, add their name to your follow-up list the next week on a different day. If you did connect with them and schedule an appointment or handle the issue, take them off of the follow-up list.

Prioritize Your Task List

You might want to assign a specific priority to each task, so you can start your day with the most important things and work your way down from there. Submitting a form would be at the bottom of the list. It needs to be done, but it's not time consuming.

I like to start off with the easy tasks. It makes me feel productive to be able to cross things off. When Mike gets into the office from 8:30am to 9:30am there may be a couple things we need to do together. And if the day is really busy I can usually find time in the afternoon to finish off any lingering to-dos. I'll tackle what I can, knowing I have some floating opportunities later on to finish things if I don't get it all done in the morning.

Bigger to-do's, like planning for appointments or creating illustrations, need to be done at least one day before. You don't want to pull something like that together on the same day. If it takes longer than you thought, or an emergency comes up and pulls your attention away from prep, suddenly you're stressed out and underprepared. Don't let that happen. Schedule a Time Block before the day of the appointment to review and prepare everything you're going to need.

When it comes to financial planning, pulling reports, conducting research, printing things off, and other time consuming activities, get them done ahead of time.

Another thing I get done well in advance is my birthday cards. I Time Block a session on my calendar at the end of each month to hand write all the birthday cards for the next month. Then I mail them all out on the same day. When I know it's going to be a birthday card day I usually get to the office early so I can spend the morning writing cards before the market opens. Then at 8:30am I'm ready to start making phone calls.

Learning how to Time Block and structure your to-do's on a daily basis will allow you to be conscious about making sure your time is utilized to 100% efficiency.

Share Your To-Dos

When Mike and I schedule individual appointments with our clients we try to place them on non-office days unless it's a joint appointment we both need to attend. This way our office days can be utilized exactly how we want with interviews, outbound business development calls, and following our Time Blocks to the T. On those days if one of us needs help with anything, we can rely on the other.

We also share our to-do lists with each other. Mike can see the people I need to follow up with and the forms I need to submit. We can rely on each other. We can also both see when there's something personal on the calendar, like if Mike and Elana have a date night or a volleyball tournament. That's a way to be transparent. We have everything written down so we can work together to get it all accomplished.

The same efficiency can be achieved in a couple or a family by sharing a to-do list. Laying out your collective goals will create feelings of cohesion and teamwork. It's a family accomplishment.

We succeed together as a firm because that's how we want it to be. Everything is shared. Everything is on the calendar. Everything is on the to-do list. We know what we need to do without even discussing it. Transparency in business makes work easier on all fronts.

Even when I was at PNC and Adam needed to schedule a call with me he could see my calendar. He knew what I had going on and he worked around it. Everybody should be transparent. Nobody should be misleading anyone else.

Simplify and Centralize

When I was at PNC I used to write down every person I was following up with and what the opportunity was on a yellow legal pad. Whenever Adam came to visit me I could show him my pad: "Here's how many people I'm following up with."

I was writing down to-do's on sticky notes as they came in. Then I'd have one bigger sticky note and write it all down there for the next day. It worked great at the office.

But I found if there was anything I didn't get done during the 9-5 period of time at the bank, I couldn't do much from home without my yellow legal pad and all of my sticky notes. I then started doing everything in Outlook. Now instead of using sticky notes and legal pads, I keep my to-dos in an open draft window.

It makes organizing easier because I always have everything with me. Also, it's more eco-friendly and I'm not wasting paper.

How I Set My Own Goals

In addition to a daily to-do list you can also have longer-term lists of tasks you plan to get done. Make monthly and annual goals for yourself, both professionally and personally. When you write them down and put them into your calendar the goals become more real.

Mike and I have a white board in our office where we write annual sales goals, hiring goals, and strategy for J.M.Equity Advisors moving forward. When we're having conversations with advisors, we talk about strategy. Every Friday we review the whiteboard and adjust our numbers. We also maintain a list of people we have in the pipeline as possible advisors.

Our business goals are always evolving and they're always top of mind. They're in our face when we're in the office. We're always being reminded of what we need to do and where we want to be.

Personally, I have yearly goals, which I make before New Years and save as a note in my phone. I'll make sure to review those at least on a weekly basis. I'll start thinking around Thanksgiving about goals I want to set myself for the next year. That way by January 1st I'm not scrambling for ideas. I'm ready to go.

Share Your To-Do List

Why not share your personal to-do list with your spouse or significant other? As a couple you can talk about what tasks need to be accomplished the next day. You can work through who's going to take which tasks. That way nothing is neglected.

It becomes a family to-do list. For example:

- pick up groceries
- get kids from school
- grab dry-cleaning
- drop off kids at basketball

It's a team accomplishment to run the errands smoothly and efficiently. It feels like these are the tasks you're going to accomplish together. By sharing this list and talking about it you are working as a team to complete the list. You'll feel at the end of the day like it was all a team accomplishment. Nothing slips through the cracks and everybody's on the same page.

It's a form of silent communication. You are being transparent to make sure everything gets done and the responsibilities don't all fall on one person. Each night you can talk about what was accomplished and what needs to get done the next day. Then you can write it all down and assign the tasks to one person or the other.

The key is when you agree to take on a task, you have to follow through. Failing to follow through will ruin trust in your relationships.

Remembering dates is something I've struggled with myself.

Every other weekend I go stay in the suburbs with Jayden and Samantha. There have been many times when she told me about things like a doctor's appointment, wedding, pickup, or drop-off in the near future that I agreed to, but then forgot about when the date came nearer.

ME: "Did we talk about this?"

SAMANTHA: "Yeah, I told you a month ago."

Several times I forgot about an event or appointment I'd agreed to handle and Samantha rightfully felt betrayed. Today, we share a to-do list and she schedules Time Blocks on my calendar whenever I need to make a pick-up or be at an appointment.

What makes the to-do list work is preparing it the day before and spending time organizing it so you can attack it the next day. It's important to do this in your personal life as well. Spend the last 30 minutes of your day organizing your personal to-do list for the next day. There are some other key things you can knock out the night before as well, in order to make yourself more productive the next day. I'll discuss that in the next chapter.

Chapter 10

The Night Before

To stay focused during the day, turn off your notifications and vibrations. That means there will be missed calls, text messages, and social media comments that you don't see as they come in. Even on silent mode, you might see notifications and respond on the fly during the day, but if they aren't urgent, you should let them go and focus on your Time Blocks and other activities that grow your business.

To make this work, it's critical to reserve some time at the end of the day to take care of those things, respond to people, and turn any appropriate tasks into to-dos. Use that time to look through your texts and social media to see who you missed so you can make sure to respond. People appreciate hearing back from you on the same day. It's easy to say, "Hey, sorry, it's been a crazy day. How about we touch base this weekend?"

Also, this can't stretch out into more than 30 minutes. You don't want to be scrambling to accomplish big important to-dos in this time before bed. For those kinds of things it's best to wake up earlier and get them done before the day starts. Once you leave work and go home it's family time.

You can leave little things that don't take much thinking, analyzing, or planning for the evening, but don't try to tackle anything big. Instead, schedule those larger to-do's for the next morning and get quality sleep. You can always wake up at 5:00am, then by 5:30am or 6:00am you're at the gym and by 7:30am you're at your desk and ready to start your work day. Now from 7:30am to 8:00am you have a half hour to accomplish those leftover to-do's and by 8:00am you can start your calls.

There's always a way to get things done. You always have time. It's a matter of structuring your day and getting it all done efficiently.

Before you leave the office each day, review your to-do's for the next day and look over all of the appointments and interviews you have scheduled. That's when you can do any prep you need to get done for the next day's appointments so when the next day arrives you're 100% ready to go. This way you can spend the next morning completing your to-do's and follow-ups instead of preparing for your appointments. You can stick to your Time Blocks and grow your business.

For me, this means before I leave the office I need to take care of things like finalizing financial plans, pulling reports, and preparing slide decks.

Some days you might have four appointments lined up in the afternoon and three scheduled in the morning. Maybe it's just one of those days. If you legitimately don't complete every task because you were too busy at the office and then you have to go catch your son's baseball game, there's still this period of time in the evening where you're lying in bed planning your day. There may be some unanswered emails you want to take care of.

There might even be small to-do's you can wrap up right there. Try spending a half hour before bed answering unanswered emails, looking over your to-do's for the next day, and making sure you didn't forget to follow up with anyone. If you're Time Blocking properly it shouldn't ever be more than an hour. I get all of this done within 15-30 minutes.

If you had a crazy day and you still have to prep for tomorrow's meetings, don't kill yourself during this time. You're exhausted and depleted at that point. Instead, focus on getting back to people and planning out how to most efficiently tackle the outstanding items tomorrow. This might be one of those days where you wake up early and be first into the office to finish up your prep work. Then adjust your Time Blocking going forward so the problem doesn't happen again.

This nightly routine shouldn't be more than a half hour. It's not a time for *doing*, it's a time for *planning*. The idea is that from the moment you wake up the next morning you'll know what you need to do, what the schedule is, what the Time Blocked activities are, and how you're going to tackle everything throughout the day.

Get Back to Everyone

No email should ever go unanswered for more than 24 hours. With any emails you couldn't get to throughout the day, you've got to get back to those people at night. And even if you don't have an answer for them you can say, "Thanks for the follow-up. And thank you for your patience. I did receive your email. These are very good questions. I will be sure to research these answers and get back to you within the next day or two." Then add it to your to-do list. This way they know you got their email and are working on an answer. Being prompt is huge. You have to be prompt with your emails.

The same is true if somebody calls you. You should always call them back within a 24 hour span. There will be times when you have a lot going on and somebody calls you or leaves a voicemail and you can't get back to them right away. At the end of the business day when you're driving home you can give them a call or shoot them a text saying, "It's been a busy day but I'm working on it. I will definitely give you a call tomorrow in the morning." You should always get back to the people within 24 hours.

Starting right after the holidays and continuing through the end of April is the busiest time for a financial advisor because it's tax time. Most people want to review their accounts in the beginning of the year to plan for the year ahead—even though I already met with them at the end of the previous year.

It's nice for people to meet with me when they're filing taxes because if they need to make any additional contributions it has to be done before taxes are filed. Or if they need any documents from me I can provide those to their accountants. It's a very busy time. When I was at PNC I would be stacked with appointments from nine to five during tax season. I wasn't eating lunch. It was back-to-back meetings all day long. A lot of my to-do's and follow-ups fell by the wayside. Then I'd have to tackle everything in the evening. Some people required urgent attention because they needed specific things for their taxes. So I had to get back to them promptly. Also, that's the time of year when a lot of people add money to their accounts, another reason to be highly attentive during that time.

People aren't going to keep hounding you every day if they haven't heard from you. They trust you're working on it. Don't break their trust.

Clients appreciate when you acknowledge you got their message and you're working on it. It's easy and allows you to get back to everyone within 24 hours, even if you don't fully respond to what they are saying.

Yesterday I got a call at 6:30pm from Easton, a client of mine, and I couldn't answer the phone. By the time I did it was 7:30pm and felt too late to call. So I shot Easton a text saying, "Hey, I saw you called, I'm sorry I missed you. I will give you a call first thing tomorrow morning. I did get your voicemail. You can expect a call from me by 8:00am." The next morning I gave Easton a call to answer some questions and it was a good touch base.

Easton said, "Thanks for getting back to me last night. I really didn't expect to hear from you being that it was 6:30pm, but thanks."

Little messages like that matter.

Like I said previously, I don't meet anybody on weekends because that's my time with Jayden. But people will still shoot me little emails with questions. So Sunday afternoon when Jayden takes a nap I'll open my laptop and get back to everyone. If I need to make a call or find some answers, I always say, "I got your email. Thanks for reaching out to me. Monday morning I'll be in the office by 8:00am. Let me get you some answers and I'll give you a call between 8:30am and 9:30am."

Nearly 90% of the time people email me back right away and say, "Oh my God, you're working on the weekend? I didn't expect you to answer this until Monday, but thank you for the follow-up. Hope all as well. Give me a call whenever you can tomorrow." It's as simple as that. People appreciate it and it takes no time.

On Sunday night I start to plan for my next day and week.

Using Nights in the Personal Sphere

What if you and your spouse committed to taking a few moments at the end of each night to lie in bed together and talk about the day? You can use this time to plan for the day ahead and review the family tasks that need to be done.

If you make this a regular routine it can serve like a team bonding experience. In five or ten minutes you're both on the same page about everything. You know what needs to be done and you're ready to divide up the tasks. You can avoid the possibility of forgetting to do something. By talking through everything you might discover more efficient ways to divide up responsibilities. "Hey, I have an appointment at the end of the day near the school so I could pick up the kids and you could stop by the store instead of me."

If you have a document where you're sharing a to-do list, that's a great thing to review together with your spouse during those 5-10 minutes. Make sure nothing slips through the cracks and nothing is missed. You can even color coordinate who's taking which items.

This way the next day you won't waste any time wondering what you need to do. You'll simply execute. With families, responsibilities get complicated. You're going to have many activities that require planning and coordination. That's why sharing a calendar, sharing to-do's, and sharing reminders is so important.

Don't Let Your Review Take Too Long

If you worked all day at the office and now you're sitting in bed on your phone during the rare few minutes of time you and your spouse have alone together, that might not go over well. You could talk about it and focus on the fact that the underlying reason for this new habit is so that you're more efficient with your time during the day and can get home in time for dinner.

That's also why it's important that your Night Before time should never be more than a half hour in length. Go through everything quickly. Set a timer for yourself. Don't linger.

If you have a hundred unread emails you might only get to 50. That means you need to set your alarm half an hour earlier the next day, get to the office sooner, and answer the rest of the emails before the day starts. Then do better with your Time Blocking tomorrow.

Everybody can take 15 minutes at the end of their day to look through what they missed and respond and provide an alternative solution if they can't finish things right then and there. Even if you're busy, reply to people within 24 hours. You can look at your calendar for the next week and suggest a time to connect.

People are going to feel appreciative to hear from you. By responding promptly you are thanking them for caring about you. Most of the time if you're busy you can find another time to touch base. But at least they don't feel forgotten about or unimportant.

That's something I need to work on in my personal life. I feel justified in pushing people off because I'm busy, but I shouldn't because everybody is busy too. Everybody has work all day and a family or significant other to deal with in the evenings. People are tired and if they're going to take the time to care about me, I need to reciprocate that.

Try adopting a brief period at the end of the day where you look back through your personal messages and at least get back to everyone with a very brief text. This has been working really well for me. People like seeing that even though I'm busy I made it a priority to reach out to them in the evening before bed and let them know I saw their message and will get back to them when I can.

Those are the basic components of Meat Around the Bone Communication, and how to implement them in your personal and professional life. In the next chapter, I'll show you how to put it all together and get started.

Chapter 11
It's Go Time

Are you ready to put some Meat Around the Bone? Are you ready to apply these communication principles to your personal and professional relationships? The way you conduct yourself personally is going to bleed into your business and professional life. In order to achieve complete happiness you need to focus on both sides of the picture.

When I got hired at Edward Jones their mentality was that we should knock on as many doors and talk to as many people as we possibly could. They trained us on what to say when people answered the door, and that was it. We learned that as long as you knock on 1,000 doors, you'll get at least 1 sale. It's a numbers game.

But what about the other 999 people you talked to? Maybe some of them told you, "I'll think about it," or said, "Can you send me some stuff?" Nurture those relationships and you can close sales. Implement good follow up or else leads will fall through the cracks.

This book is about how to implement those activities both personally and professionally. You can read it differently depending on what phase of life you're in. Take what you want from it.

Even the most successful people are always going to be reading the latest book looking for ways to improve themselves.

I hope this book has made you think about how to constantly touch the important people in your life. I hope you've gotten some ideas about how you can Fatten Up your relationships and Maintain the Muscle Mass going forward.

It starts with little steps and some experimenting, and once you start applying them consistently they turn into habits. Pick a few strategies to focus on and start applying them to your life. Do them until they become automatic and you'll see a massive shift in your relationships.

Not only will Meat Around the Bone Communication help you in your career and enable you to close more deals, it's going to influence the way you think about your relationships at home too. The simple skills and behaviors I've outlined here can help overcome divorce, prevent break-ups, and reduce confrontation. It starts with little things, but they add up to much more.

At the end of the day, this book is about more than you. It's about your family. It's about the actions you take on a daily basis in all areas of your life. Nobody wants their son or daughter to grow up hearing, "Your dad is pretty successful but he's an asshole." No kid needs that. So this is much bigger than you. It directly impacts everyone around you moving forward.

Go through this book one chapter at a time, review each principle, and write down a few people in your life who you could apply that principle with. Think about your business and your life and look for opportunities to improve. And if you struggle with that, ask other people like your co-workers, boss, significant other, siblings, children, and friends. You'll certainly get feedback.

Sit down and think about these things. You can't rush self-discovery.

As you make progress, the other people in your life will see what you're up to. They will notice you working on improving. Your kids are going to see it. They're going to see you and your spouse getting along better and arguing less. They'll see you all starting to do things as a family and spend more time together.

When kids see healthy and open communication between their parents, it makes them feel safe opening up. I want Jayden to be able to tell me things and talk to me when he has issues. I don't want him to keep it inside, afraid to open up because he sees how I communicate with other adults.

So analyze your own life. What successes have you had? Where can you expand that success? What areas of opportunity are there? What would complete success and happiness look like for you, your family, and your kids?

It's bigger than you. These small changes can impact everyone in your life.

And once you do start to implement them, monitor your progress. Did the changes result in more positive conversations and deeper personal relationships? It's important to look carefully at whether or not the things you're doing are working.

If changes are not working, what could be the problem? Are you Time Blocking? Do you have a system for follow-ups? Are you dedicating enough time to business-growing activities? What are you doing, and is it working? You can measure in different ways.

Hold yourself accountable and watch as the changes start to stack up. When you fix this stuff, you're on your way. Once that happens, this book did exactly what it was supposed to do. Good for you.

At the same time, don't be too hard on yourself. Affirm yourself when you make progress, even if you aren't changing everything all at once. If you talked to your significant other about your feelings, for example, notice that and affirm yourself. That's an improvement. You're on the journey. You have made some major progress by getting to the point where you recognize what you need to improve. That was a two year process for me!

One easy place to start is to implement nightly check-ins with your significant other to talk about the next day, hear each other's calendars, and share to-do's. That can start immediately. There's no reason not to do that. Anyone reading this book can instantly open their calendar and start Time Blocking activities like that.

When you take this moment at night to check in with your partner about everything that needs to be done the next day, your partner will think, *Wow, this is different, he's trying to communicate with me.* And it's something very small. It doesn't take a lot of time.

Start implementing little things and gradually build up to bigger things. Be true to your own circumstances and comfort level.

Some people might want to try and change multiple areas of their lives at one time. Others might prefer to focus on a single area in a more concentrated way. That's where sitting down and analyzing yourself is important. How are you going to get it all done?

Somebody going through divorce or dealing with debt might

want to implement more of these strategies than somebody who is trying to communicate better. A rapid pace of change can be sustainable when it comes from a Moment of Recharacterization. When you change your idea of who you are it becomes possible to radically shift your behavior overnight.

A new you is waiting. A you that communicates with Meat Around the Bone and makes everyone in your life feel special, without ending up tired and depleted at the end of each day. All you have to do is make the decision.

www.ingramcontent.com/pod-product-compliance
Lightning Source LLC
Chambersburg PA
CBHW060917140726
47996CB00001B/278